MANY
LONG YEARS AGO

OGDEN NASH

Many
Long
Years
Ago

BOSTON

LITTLE, BROWN AND COMPANY

FOR N. J. L

In June of 1931
She gained a moody, broody son,
While he acquired, with loud hurrah,
A calm and understanding ma.
Because she never tried to change him,
Reform, reprove or re-arrange him,
But gave him only love and wisdom,
And in her kingdom freedom was hisdom,
In '45 he can but purr
And dedicate this book to her.

CONTENTS

· x ·

· xi ·

· xv ·

CONTENTS

· xi ·

· xv ·

MANY
LONG YEARS AGO

Just imagine yourself seated on a shadowy terrace,

And beside you is a girl who stirs you more strangely
than an heiress.

It is a summer evening at its most superb,

And the moonlight reminds you that To Love is an
active verb,

And your hand clasps hers, which rests there without
shrinking,

And after a silence fraught with romance you ask her
what she is thinking,

And she starts and returns from the moon-washed distances to the shadowy veranda,

And says, Oh I was wondering how many bamboo
shoots a day it takes to feed a baby Giant Panda.

Or you stand with her on a hilltop and gaze on a winter
sunset,

And everything is as starkly beautiful as a page from
Sigrid Undset,

And your arm goes round her waist and you make an
avowal which for masterfully marshaled emotional
content might have been a page of Ouida's or
Thackeray's,

And after a silence fraught with romance she says, I
forgot to order the limes for the Daiquiris.

Or in a twilight drawing room you have just asked the
most momentous of questions,

And after a silence fraught with romance she says, I
think this little table would look better where that

little table is, but then where would that little
table go, have you any suggestions?
And that's the way they go around hitting below our
belts;
It isn't that nothing is sacred to them, it's just that at
the Sacred Moment they are always thinking of
something else.

A BAS BEN ADHEM

My fellow man I do not care for.
I often ask me, What's he there for?
The only answer I can find
Is, Reproduction of his kind.
If I'm supposed to swallow that,
Winnetka is my habitat.
Isn't it time to carve Hic Jacet
Above that Reproduction racket?

To make the matter more succinct:
Suppose my fellow man extinct.
Why, who would not approve the plan
Save possibly my fellow man?
Yet with a politician's voice
He names himself as Nature's choice.

The finest of the human race
Are bad in figure, worse in face.
Yet just because they have two legs
And come from storks instead of eggs
They count the spacious firmament
As something to be charged and sent.

Though man created smocks and snoods
And one-way streets and breakfast foods,
And double features and mustard plasters,
And Andrews Sisters and Lady Astors,
He hails himself with drum and fife
And bullies lower forms of life.

· 5 ·

Not that I think that much depends
On how we treat our feathered friends,
Or claim the wart hog in the zoo
Is nearer God than me or you;
Just that I wonder, as I scan,
The wherefore of my fellow man.

SEASIDE SERENADE

It begins when you smell a funny smell,
And it isn't vanilla or caramel,
And it isn't forget-me-nots or lilies,
Or new-mown hay, or daffy-down-dillies,
And it's not what the barber rubs on Father,
And it's awful, and yet you like it rather.
No, it's not what the barber rubs on Daddy,
It's more like an elderly finnan haddie,
Or, shall we say, an electric fan
Blowing over a sardine can.
It smells of seaweed, it smells of clams,
It's as fishy as first-night telegrams,
It's as fishy as millions of fishy fishes,
In spite of which you find it delishes,
You could do with a second helping, please,
And that, my dears, is the ocean breeze.
And pretty soon you observe a pack
Of people reclining upon their back,
And another sight that is very common
Is people reclining upon their abdomen.
And now you lose the smell of the ocean
In the sweetish vapor of sunburn lotion,
And the sun itself seems paler and colder,
Compared to vermilion face and shoulder.
Athletic young men uncover their torso
In the virile way that maidens adore so,
While paunchy uncles, before they bathe them,
In voluminous beach robes modestly swathe them.

The beach is peppered with ladies who look
Like pictures out of a medical book.
Last, not least, consider the kiddies,
Chirping like crickets and Katydiddies,
Splashing, squealing, slithering, crawling,
Cheerful, tearful, boisterous, bawling,
Kiddies in clamorous crowds that swarm
Heavily over your prostrate form,
Callous kiddies who gallop in myriads
'Twixt ardent Apollos and eager Nereids,
Kiddies who bring, as a priceless cup,
Something dead that a wave washed up.
Well, it's each to his taste, and a taste to each;
Shall we saunter down to the bathing beach?

SEDATIVE REFLECTION

Let the love-lorn lover cure insomnia
By murmuring AMOR VINCIT OMNIA.

Some people are popular with other people because
their wit is pointed
And they can sing tenor and are double-jointed
And have had experiences in the Shetlands and the
Hebrides
And have private anecdotes about public celebrides,
And are bright and amusing in the entr'acte
And always do the right thing in backgammon and
centr'acte.

Other people are unpopular with other people because
they discuss Bertrand Russell
And keep wanting you to feel their muscle
And point out that your furniture is oak, not mahogany,
And tell you all about their ancestors and progeny
And advise you to move to a suburb
And get away from all this tumult and huburb.

Both kinds of people, however, will eventually succumb
to acidity;
Or perhaps they will be victims of the humidity
Or even approach metempsychosis
Through the various stages of cirrhosis.
But whatever the manner of their passing may be
It's all all right with me.

NEVERTHELESS

I am not fond of Oliver Montrose.
Oliver is a person I despise;
The purple veins that bulbify his nose,
The crimson veins that irrigate his eyes.
His wheezy breath his vinous weakness shows;
He is the slave of whisky, beer and gin.
I am not fond of Oliver Montrose;
I hate the sinner. But what a warming sin!

Bibesco Poolidge is a man of jowl;
I've never seen a dewlap, but on him;
He shines with the grease of many a basted fowl;
Ten thousand sauces round his innards swim.
The ghosts of hosts of kine about him prowl,
Lamb, pig, and game blood trickles from his chin;
I cannot look on him without a scowl;
I hate the sinner. But what a luscious sin!

I do not dote on Murgatroyd Van Rust,
So tasty to the tenderest of genders.
Practically everything that has a bust
Surveys his suave ensemble and surrenders.
The way he parts his hair I do not trust;
Let the phone ring, I loathe his knowing grin.
You cannot see his diary for the dust,
I hate the sinner. Still, if one had to sin . . .

O Mammonites and spendthrifts, draw ye nigh,
Fingernail-biters and sluggards, come on in,
Consider now how tolerant am I
Who hate the sinner, yet who love the sin.

WHEN THE DEVIL WAS SICK COULD
HE PROVE IT?

Few things are duller
Than feeling unspecifically off-color,
Yes, you feel like the fulfilment of a dismal prophecy,
And you don't feel either exercisey or officey,
But still you can't produce a red throat or a white
    tongue or uneasy respiration or any kind of a
    symptom,
And it is very embarrassing that whoever was supposed
    to be passing out the symptoms skymptom,
Because whatever is the matter with you, you can't
    spot it
But whatever it is, you've got it,
But the question is how to prove it,
And you suck for hours on the mercury of the ther-
    mometer you finally sent out for and you can't
    move it,
And your entire system may be pneumococci'd or
    streptococci'd,
But the looks you get from your loved ones are simply
    skepticocci'd,
And Conscience glares at you in her Here comes that
    bad penny way,
Crying There's nothing the matter with you, you're
    just trying to get out of doing something you never
    wanted to do anyway,
So you unfinger your pulse before Conscience can jeer
    at you for a fingerer,

And you begin to believe that perhaps she is right,
     perhaps you are nothing but a hypochondriacal old
     malingerer,
And you take a farewell look at the thermometer,
And that's when you hurl the bometer.
Yes sir, it's as good as a tonic,
Because you've got as pretty a ninety-nine point one as
     you'd wish to see in a month of bubonic.
Some people hold out for a hundred or more before
     they collapse
But that leaves too many gaps;
As for me,
I can get a very smug Monday, Tuesday, Wednesday,
     Thursday, or Friday in bed out of a tenth of a
     degree.
It is to this trait that I am debtor
For the happy fact that on week ends I generally feel
     better.

Sing me a song of city summers,
And I will parry with mine;
Pledge me in praise
Of these halcyon days,
And I will yammer for wine.
Say me a word about Manhattan,
The health resort supreme —
I haste to reply
That you and I
Will never grow intime.

For I and the thermometer
Are living in the Eighties,
The semi-tropic Eighties
That the sun refuses to set on.
And through the open windows
Ooze the Franks and Bings and Katies
And all the other tonsileers
The sponsors lavishly bet on.

Tell me again of urban coolth,
And I'll love you like a measle.
Just one remark
About Central Park,
And friendship pops like a weasel.
Comfort me not with tales of heat waves
Shimmering o'er Syosset;
What boots it to me
In 11 B
With my forehead under the faucet?

For I am in the Eighties,
But the thermometer's in the Nineties,
The hotsy-totsy Nineties,
Where the creditor melts with the debtor,
Where humidity assembles
In gallons, quarts and pinties,
And the White Rock boils in the icebox,
And the settee sticks to the setter.

Come, say you envy my airy flat,
Free of the country's trammels.
They select your end,
My chirrupy friend,
You've a date at Frank E. Campbell's.
Oh, who with a ten-mile trip in view
Wouldn't rather ride than hike it?
So in town I pause
For financial cause,
But I'm damned if I'll say I like it.

For I and the thermometer,
Are living in the Eighties,
The East-of-Lexington Eighties
Where the best resembles the worst.
And the kiddies in the street
Bark like crocodiles in the Euphrates,
And I wonder what Pippa and Pollyanna would say
If our positions became reversed.

THE CAT

You get a wife, you get a house,
Eventually you get a mouse.
You get some words regarding mice,
You get a kitty in a trice.
By two A.M., or thereabout,
The mouse is in, the cat is out.
It dawns upon you, in your cot,
The mouse is silent, the cat is not.
Instead of Pussy, says your spouse,
You should have bought another mouse.

OH, STOP BEING THANKFUL ALL OVER
THE PLACE

In the glittering collection of paste diamonds one in
    particular ranks very high,
And that is the often-quoted remark of the prominent
    and respectable dignitary who on seeing a con-
    demned man on his way to the scaffold crashed into
    a thousand anthologies by remarking, There but for
    the grace of God go I.
Here is a deplorable illustration
Of sloppy ratiocination;
Here is a notable feat
Of one-way thinking on a two-way street.
It must certainly have been the speaker's lucky day,
Or otherwise he would have been run over by his
    speech turning around and coming back the other
    way,
Because did he stop to work out his premise to its
    logical conclusion? Ah no,
He just got it off and let it go,
And now whenever people are with people they want
    to impress with their combined greatheartedness
    and book-learning they cry
Oh look at that condemned man on his way to the
    scaffold, there but for the grace of God go I.
Which is so far so good, but they neglect to continue
    with the heretofore unspoken balance of the theme,
    which is equally true,
That there but for the grace of God goes Jimmie

Durante or the Prince of Wales or Aimee Semple
McPherson or Dr. Wellington Koo,

Or Moses or Napoleon or Cleopatra or King Midas,

Or a man named Harris who is just getting over an
attack of tonsilidas.

So away with you, all you parrot-like repeaters of high-
sounding phrases that you never stop to consider
what they actually mean,

I wouldn't allow you to stay in any college of which I
was the Dean.

I can never listen to you without thinking Oh my,

There but for the grace of God speak I.

Anxious Parent, I guess you have just never been
   around;
I guess you just don't know who are the happiest peo-
   ple anywhere to be found;
So you are worried, are you, because your child is turn-
   ing out to be phlegmatic?
Forgive me if I seem a trifle unsympathatic.
Why do you want your child to be a flashing, cor-
   uscating gem?
Don't you know the only peace the world can give
   lies not in flame but in phlegm?
Don't you know that the people with souls of putty
Are the only people who are sitting prutty?
They never get all worked up at the drop of a pin or
   a feather or a hat,
They never go around saying bitterly to themselves:
   "Oh God, did I really do, did I really say that?"
They never boil over when they read about stool pigeons
   getting girls into reformatories by making treacher-
   ous advances;
They never get perfectly futilely harrowed about Sacco
   and Vanzetti, or Alice Adamses who don't have
   good times at dances;
They never blink an eyelash about colleges that are
   going to the dogs because of football overem-
   phasis;
They never almost die with indignation when some

colored person is lynched in Natchez or Memphasis.

No, when they eat they digest their food, and when they go to bed they get right to sleep,

And four phlegmatic angels a stolid watch over them keep.

Oh to be phlegmatic, oh to be stolid, oh to be torpid, Oh to be calm!

For it is only thus, Anxious Parent, that we can get through life without a qualm.

Vanity, vanity, all is vanity
That's any fun at all for humanity.
Food is vanity, so is drink,
And undergarments of gossamer pink,
S. J. Perelman, long vacations,
Going abroad, and rich relations,
The kind of engagements you want to keep,
A hundred honors, and twelve hours' sleep.
Vanities all — Oh Worra, worra!
Rooted in Sodom and Gomorrah.

Vanity, vanity, all is vanity
That's any fun at all for humanity.
That is the gist of the prophet's case,
From Bishop Cannon to Canon Chase.
The prophets chant and the prophets chatter,
But somehow it never seems to matter,
For the world hangs on to its ancient sanity
And orders another round of vanity.
Then Hey! for Gomorrah! and Nonny! for Sodom!
Marie! the Chanel model for Modom!

THE PARTY

Come Arabella, fetch the cake,
On a dish with silver handles.
Oh mercy! Feel the table shake!
Lucinda, light the candles.

For Mr. Migg is thir–ty,
Is thir——ty,
Is thir———ty.
The years are crawling over him
Like wee red ants.
Oh, three times ten is thir–ty,
Is for——ty,
Is fif———ty.
The further off from England
The nearer is to France.

The little flames they bob and jig,
The dining hall is breezy.
Quick! puff your candles, Mr. Migg,
The little flames die easy.
For Mr. Migg is for–ty,
Is for——ty,
Is for———ty.
The years are crawling over him
Like wee red ants.
Oh four times ten is for–ty,
Is fif——ty,
Is six———ty,

And creeping through the icing,
The other years advance.

Why, Arabella, here's a ring!
Lucinda, here's a thimble!
For Mr. Migg there's not a thing —
'Tis not, I trust, a symbol!

For Mr. Migg is fif–ty,
Is fif——ty,
Is fif———ty.
The years are crawling over him
Like wee red ants.
Oh, five times ten is fif–ty,
Is six——ty,
Is seven———ty.
Lucinda, put the cake away.
We're going to the dance.

BENJAMIN

There was a brave girl of Connecticut
Who flagged the express with her pecticut,
Which critics defined
As presence of mind,
But deplorable absence of ecticut.

I hardly suppose I know anybody who wouldn't rather
be a success than a failure,

Just as I suppose every piece of crabgrass in the garden
would much rather be an azalea,

And in celestial circles all the run-of-the-mill angels
would rather be archangels or at least cherubim
and seraphim,

And in the legal world all the little process-servers hope
to grow up into great big bailiffim and sheriffim.

Indeed, everybody wants to be a wow,

But not everybody knows exactly how.

Some people think they will eventually wear diamonds
instead of rhinestones

Only by everlastingly keeping their noses to their ghrine-
stones,

And other people think they will be able to put in more
time at Palm Beach and the Ritz

By not paying too much attention to attendance at
the office but rather in being brilliant by starts and
fits.

Some people after a full day's work sit up all night getting a college education by correspondence,

While others seem to think they'll get just as far by
devoting their evenings to the study of the difference in temperament between brunettance and
blondance.

In short, the world is filled with people trying to achieve
success,

And half of them think they'll get it by saying No and
    half of them by saying Yes,
And if all the ones who say No said Yes, and vice versa,
    such is the fate of humanity that ninety-nine per
    cent of them still wouldn't be any better off than
    they were before,
Which perhaps is just as well because if everybody was
    a success nobody could be contemptuous of any-
    body else and everybody would start in all over
    again trying to be a bigger success than everybody
    else so they would have somebody to be contemptu-
    ous of and so on forevermore,
Because when people start hitching their wagons to a
    star,
That's the way they are.

THE PASSIONATE PAGAN AND THE
DISPASSIONATE PUBLIC

A TRAGEDY OF THE MACHINE AGE

Boys and girls,
Come out to play,
The moon is shining
Bright as day.

If the moon is shining
Bright as day,
We think that we'll
Stay in and play.

Hey nonny nonny!
Come, Jennie! Come, Johnnie!
The year's adolescent!
The air's effervescent!
It bubbles like Schweppes!
Aren't you going to take steppes?

It's one of the commoner
Vernal phenomena.
You may go wild
Over air that is mild,
But Johnnie and Jennie
Are not having any.

It is Spring! It is Spring!
Let us leap! Let us sing!

Let us claim we have hives
And abandon our wives!
Let us hire violins
To encourage our sins!
Let us loll in a grotto!
Let this be our motto:
Not sackcloth, but satin!
Not Nordic, but Latin!

An epicene voice
Is our amorous choice!
Tell us that Luna
Compares with that cruna.
Away with your capers!
Go peddle your papers!

It is Spring! It is Spring!
On the lea, on the ling!
The frost is dispersed!
Like the buds let us burst!
Let the sap in our veins
Rush like limited trains!
Let our primitive urges
Disgruntle our clergies,
While Bacchus and Pan
Cavort in the van!

Spring is what winter
Always goes inter.
Science finds reasons
For mutable seasons.

Can't you control
That faun in your soul?
Please go and focus
Your whims on a crocus.

It is Spring! Is it Spring?
Let us sing! Shall we sing?
On the lea, on the ling
Shall we sing it is Spring?
Will nobody fling
A garland to Spring?
Oh, hey nonny nonny!
Oh, Jennie! Oh, Johnnie!
Doesn't dove rhyme with love
While the moon shines above?
Isn't May for the wooer
And June for l'amour?
No, it couldn't be Spring!
Do not dance! Do not sing!
These birds and these flowers,
These breezes and bowers,
These gay tirra-lirras
Are all done with mirrors!
Hey nonny! Hey nonny!
Hey nonny! Hey nonny!
Hey nonny! Hey nonny!
Hey nonny . . .

THEATRICAL REFLECTION

In the Vanities
No one wears panities.

PORTRAIT OF THE ARTIST AS A
PREMATURELY OLD MAN

It is common knowledge to every schoolboy and even
    every Bachelor of Arts,

That all sin is divided into two parts.

One kind of sin is called a sin of commission, and that
    is very important,

And it is what you are doing when you are doing some-
    thing you ortant,

And the other kind of sin is just the opposite and is
    called a sin of omission and is equally bad in the
    eyes of all right-thinking people, from Billy Sunday
    to Buddha,

And it consists of not having done something you
    shuddha.

I might as well give you my opinion of these two kinds
    of sin as long as, in a way, against each other we
    are pitting them,

And that is, don't bother your head about sins of com-
    mission because however sinful, they must at least
    be fun or else you wouldn't be committing them.

It is the sin of omission, the second kind of sin,

That lays eggs under your skin.

The way you get really painfully bitten

Is by the insurance you haven't taken out and the checks
    you haven't added up the stubs of and the ap-
    pointments you haven't kept and the bills you
    haven't paid and the letters you haven't written.

Also, about sins of omission there is one particularly
    painful lack of beauty,
Namely, it isn't as though it had been a riotous red-
    letter day or night every time you neglected to do
    your duty;
You didn't get a wicked forbidden thrill
Every time you let a policy lapse or forgot to pay a
    bill;
You didn't slap the lads in the tavern on the back and
    loudly cry Whee,
Let's all fail to write just one more letter before we go
    home, and this round of unwritten letters is on me.
No, you never get any fun
Out of the things you haven't done,
But they are the things that I do not like to be amid,
Because the suitable things you didn't do give you a
    lot more trouble than the unsuitable things you
    did.
The moral is that it is probably better not to sin at all,
    but if some kind of sin you must be pursuing,
Well, remember to do it by doing rather than by not
    doing.

Gentlemen, I give you the British Empire,
And the late Queen Victoria, by no means a vempire.
Britain and Britons I far from excoriate,
I deeply admire their Poet Laureate,
I prefer an evening with A. P. Herbert
To a sail in the moonlight sipping sherbert,
And I'd rather hear a Savoy opera
Than loll in the tropics cornering copra,
And I think Miss Lillie is quite a card
And I'm all agog over Scotland Yard.
I'm impressed by squires who run for Parliament
And serve their country for a modest emolument.
Yes, I praise their peers and I praise their commoners,
Their fogs and faces and other phenomenas;
I'm even sufficiently flibberty-gibberty
To praise their premise of personal liberty.
But bo, I'll hand you the whole shebang
When they start to sling Amurrican slang,
And calculate you will lose your lunch
When you glim an Amurrican joke in Punch
For Piccadilly is less spectacular
Than its torture of Transatlantic vernacular.
Then, Bravo, Britain! and Long Live George!
Away with Yorktown and Valley Forge;
I've a spilth of open-mouthed admiration
For a top-hole pukka sahib nation
But nix on our chatter — it can't be did.
Twenty-three, skiddoo! — Yours,

                         The Candy Kid.

In New York beautiful girls can become more beautiful
    by going to Elizabeth Arden
And getting stuff put on their faces and waiting for it
    to harden,
And poor girls with nothing to their names but a letter
    or two can get rich and joyous
From a brief trip to their loyous.
So I can say with impunity
That New York is a city of opportunity.
It also has many fine theaters and hotels,
And a lot of taxis, buses, subways and els,
Best of all, if you don't show up at the office or at a
    tea nobody will bother their head,
They will just think you are dead.
That's why I really think New York is exquisite.
And someday I'm going to pay it a visit.

Once there was a poem, and it wasn't by Edgar A.
  Guest,
And it said children ought to agree like little birdies in
  their nest.
Oh forsooth forsooth!
That poem was certainly more poetry than truth,
Because do you believe that little birdies in their nest
  agree?
It doesn't sound very probable to me.
Ah no, but I can tell you what does sound probable,
And that is that life in a nest is just one long quarrel
  and squabbable.
Look at that young mother robin over in that elm, or
  is it a beech,
She has two little robins and she thinks she has solved
  her problem because she has learned not to bring
  home just one worm but a worm for each.
She is very pleased with her understanding of fledgling
  psychology, but in just about two minutes she is
  going to lose a year's growth,
Because she's going to find that one little robin gets no
  worms and the other little robin gets both,
And if one little robin gets out of the nest on the
  wrong side and nothing can please it,
Why the other little robin will choose that moment
  to tease it,
And if one little robin starts a game the other little
  robin will stop it,

And if one little robin builds a castle the other little
    robin will knock it down and if one little robin
    blows a bubble the other little robin will pop it.
Yes, I bet that if you walked up to any nest and got a
    good revealing glimpse,
Why, you would find that our little feathered friend-
    lets disagree just like human imps,
And I also bet that their distracted feathered parents
    quote feathered poetry to them by whoever the
    most popular feathered poet may be,
All about why don't they like little children in their
    nurseries agree.
Well, to put the truth about youth in a very few words,
Why the truth is that little birds do agree like children
    and children do agree like little birds,
Because you take offspring, and I don't care whether
    a house or a tree is their abode,
They may love each other but they aren't going to
    agree with each other anywhere except in an ode.
It doesn't seem to have occurred to the poet,
That nobody agrees with anybody else anyhow, but
    adults conceal it and infants show it.

THE PIG

The pig, if I am not mistaken,
Supplies us sausage, ham, and bacon.
Let others say his heart is big —
I call it stupid of the pig.

Oh Mademoiselle from Armentières,
I've heard a good deal about your affair.
Your private life, if there was a such,
From what I can gather, beat the Dutch.
At bachelor dinners and sales conventions,
You're always good for a couple of mentions.
Your quaintly distributed avoirdupois
Wrings golden chords from the locker-room boys,
And your loves are lilted in tilèd places
By whisky tenors and bacardi basses,
And soapy he-men ribaldly roar
Your affaires de coeur and affaires de corps,
Till I know your history through and through,
With a hinky dinky parlez vous.
I know your history all too well,
O Armentièrian Mademoiselle,
And I would that you'd been, if not less luscious,
At least a little more surreptutious.
It's not, dear lady, that I'm a prude,
Or frown on an amorous interlude,
But the wife, the widow, and even the maid,
At times, methinks, must pull down the shade,
Or live forever in drunken ballads
Bawled by men who are not Sir Galahads.
So, Mademoiselle, I'm tired of you
With a hinky dinky parlez vous.
I wish you had been a London spinster
With no boy friends at all but the Archbishop of
     Westminster.

LINES TO A WORLD-FAMOUS POET WHO FAILED TO COMPLETE A WORLD-FAMOUS POEM

or

COME CLEAN, MR. GUEST!

Oft when I'm sitting without anything to read waiting
    for a train in a depot,
I torment myself with the poet's dictum that to make
    a house a home, livin' is what it takes a heap o'.
Now, I myself should very much enjoy makin' my house
    a home, but my brain keeps on a-goin' clickety-
    click, clickety-click, clickety-click,
If Peter Piper picked a peck o' heap o' livin,' what kind
    of a peck o' heap o' livin' would Peter Piper pick?
Certainly a person doesn't need the brains of a Lincoln
To know that there are many kinds o' livin', just as
    there are many kinds o' dancin' or huntin' or
    fishin' or eatin' or drinkin'.
A philosophical poet should be specific
As well as prolific,
And I trust I am not being offensive
If I suggest that he should also be comprehensive.
You may if you like verify my next statement by send-
    ing a stamped, self-addressed envelope to either
    Dean Inge or Dean Gauss,
But meanwhile I ask you to believe that it takes a heap
    of other things besides a heap o' livin' to make a
    home out of a house.
To begin with, it takes a heap o' payin',
And you don't pay just the oncet, but agayin and agayin
    and agayin.

Buyin' a stock is called speculatin' and buyin' a house
is called investin',
But the value of the stock or of the house fluctuates up
and down, generally down, just as an irresponsible
Destiny may destine.
Something else that your house takes a heap o', whether
the builder came from Sicily or Erin,
Is repairin',
In addition to which, gentle reader, I am sorry to say
you are little more than an imbecile or a cretin
If you think it doesn't take a heap o' heatin',
And unless you're spiritually allied to the little Dutch
boy who went around inspectin' dikes lookin' for
leaks to put his thumb in,
It takes a heap o' plumbin',
And if it's a house that you're hopin' to spend not just
today but tomorrow in,
It takes a heap o' borrowin'.
In a word, Macushla,
There's a scad o' things that to make a house a home
it takes not only a heap, or a peck, but at least a
bushela.

NUPTIAL REFLECTION

The reason for much matrimony
Is patrimony.

Love is a word that is constantly heard,
Hate is a word that's not.
Love, I am told, is more precious than gold,
Love, I have read, is hot.
But hate is the verb that to me is superb,
And love is a drug on the mart.
Any kiddie in school can love like a fool,
But hating, my boy, is an art.

Oh, you and I and many others
Love our sweethearts and our mothers,
Love our spouses, love our tots,
Ship our love in carload lots —
Parsley, parsnips, Golden Buck,
Baked Alaska, Bombay Duck,
Sunup, sundown, sunray lamps,
Sporting prints or postage stamps,
Persimmons, even good persimmons,
Lifted faces, fallen womens,
Woes of Little Orphan Annie
Merry japes about the fanny —
Not a topic named above
That countless millions do not love.
Something somewhere's bound to pop.
I for one suggest we stop.

Hate is a word that is given the bird,
Love is the word that's lauded.

Hate, people say, is completely passé,
Vulgar, my dear, and saudid.
The atmosphere swoons with amorous tunes,
Like turtle dove calling to dove.
We are fairly discreet about what we eat,
But boy! are we gluttons in love!
Oh, fellow countrymen and others,
Turn, I beg, upon your mothers.
No more nonsense from your tots;
Teach them early what are whats.
Learn, before it grows too late,
Fellow countrymen, to hate.
Learn to hate banana salads,
Travel movies, cowboy ballads,
Literati, early risers,
Office-holders, advertisers,
Fruit-juice cocktails, borrowed wit,
Ladies who rely on It;
And fall, I pray, on yonder crooner,
Stuff his mouth with goona-goona.
Develop all your latent phobias,
And heaven's blessings will be copious.

One bliss for which
There is no match
Is when you itch
To up and scratch.

Yet doctors and dowagers deprecate scratching,
Society ranks it with spitting and snatching,
And medical circles consistently hold
That scratching's as wicked as feeding a cold.
Hell's flame burns unquenched 'neath how many a
    stocking
On account of to scratch in a salon is shocking!
Avid ankles deprived of the fingernail's kiss
For fear of a dermatological hiss!

'Neath tile or thatch
That man is rich
Who has a scratch
For every itch.

Ho, squirmers and writhers, how long will ye suffer
The medical tyrant, the social rebuffer!
On the edge of the door let our shoulderblades rub,
Let the drawing room now be as free as the tub!
Let us scratch in the presence of multitudes medical
And if they object, let us call them unedical!
So the ogres of ivy and ringworm and allergies
We'll scratch to the stature of abject apologies!

I'm greatly attached
To Barbara Frietchie.
I bet she scratched
When she was itchy.

THE COBRA

This creature fills its mouth with venum
And walks upon its duodenum.
He who attempts to tease the cobra
Is soon a sadder he, and sobra.

One thing that literature would be greatly the better for
Would be a more restricted employment by authors of
     simile and metaphor.
Authors of all races, be they Greeks, Romans, Teutons
     or Celts,
Can't seem just to say that anything is the thing it is
     but have to go out of their way to say that it is like
     something else.
What does it mean when we are told
That the Assyrian came down like a wolf on the fold?
In the first place, George Gordon Byron had had enough
     experience
To know that it probably wasn't just one Assyrian, it
     was a lot of Assyrians.
However, as too many arguments are apt to induce
     apoplexy and thus hinder longevity,
We'll let it pass as one Assyrian for the sake of brevity.
Now then, this particular Assyrian, the one whose co-
     horts were gleaming in purple and gold,
Just what does the poet mean when he says he came
     down like a wolf on the fold?
In heaven and earth more than is dreamed of in our
     philosophy there are a great many things,
But I don't imagine that among them there is a wolf
     with purple and gold cohorts or purple and gold
     anythings.
No, no, Lord Byron, before I'll believe that this As-

syrian was actually like a wolf I must have some
   kind of proof;
Did he run on all fours and did he have a hairy tail and
   a big red mouth and big white teeth and did he
   say Woof woof?
Frankly I think it very unlikely, and all you were en-
   titled to say, at the very most,
Was that the Assyrian cohorts came down like a lot of
   Assyrian cohorts about to destroy the Hebrew host.
But that wasn't fancy enough for Lord Byron, oh dear
   me no, he had to invent a lot of figures of speech
   and then interpolate them,
With the result that whenever you mention Old Testa-
   ment soldiers to people they say Oh yes, they're
   the ones that a lot of wolves dressed up in gold
   and purple ate them.
That's the kind of thing that's being done all the time
   by poets, from Homer to Tennyson;
They're always comparing ladies to lilies and veal to
   venison,
And they always say things like that the snow is a white
   blanket after a winter storm.
Oh it is, is it, all right then, you sleep under a six-inch
   blanket of snow and I'll sleep under a half-inch
   blanket of unpoetical blanket material and we'll
   see which one keeps warm,
And after that maybe you'll begin to comprehend dimly
What I mean by too much metaphor and simile.

Dear George, behold the portentous day
When bachelorhood is put away.
Bring camphor balls and cedarwood
For George's discarded bachelorhood;
You, as the happiest of men,
Wish not to wear it ever again.
Well, if you wish to get your wish,
Mark well my words, nor reply Tush-pish.
Today we fly, tomorrow we fall,
And lawyers make bachelors of us all.
If you desire a noisy nursery
And a golden wedding anniversary,
Scan first the bog where thousands falter:
They think the wooing ends at the altar,
And boast that one triumphant procession
Has given them permanent possession.
They simply desist from further endeavor,
And assume that their brides are theirs forever.
They do not beat them, they do no wrong to them,
But they take it for granted their brides belong to them.
Oh, every trade develops its tricks,
Marriage as well as politics,
Suspense is silk and complacence is shoddy,
And no one belongs to anybody.
It is pleasant, George, and necessary
To pretend the arrangement is temporary.
Thank her kindly for favors shown;
She is the lender, and she the loan;

Nor appear to notice the gradual shift
By which the loan becomes a gift.
Strong are the couples who resort
More to courtship and less to court.
And I warn you, George, for your future good,
That ladies don't want to be understood.
Women are sphinxes, Woman has writ it;
If you understand her, never admit it.
Tell her that Helen was probably beautifuller,
Call, if you will, Penelope dutifuller,
Sheba charminger, Guinevere grander
But never admit that you understand her.
Hark to the strains of Lohengrin!
Heads up, George! Go in and win!

PLATITUDINOUS REFLECTION

A good deal of superciliousness
Is based on biliousness.
People seem to be proud as peacocks
Of any infirmity, be it hives or dementia praecox

YOU CAD, WHY DON'T YOU CRINGE?

"Like most knaves he was a coward at heart . . ."
      The Thirteenth Chime, by T. C. H. Jacobs, p. 94.
"Like most knaves he was a coward at heart . . ."
                                          Ibid., p. 238.

If wishes were horses every panhandler would handle
      his pan while urging a fiery steed on,
And if turnips were watches they'd make as good eating
      as turnips, which in the first place are about as
      appetizing as watches to feed on,
And if most knaves were cowards at heart
Everything would be as simple as Mr. T. C. H. Jacobs's
      art.
Ah, if none but the good were brave,
How well would the bad behave!
Yes, if none but the bad were poltroons
Life for the good would be all cakes and ale and ice
      cream and macaroons,
And the world would be less hag-ridden,
And the air-waves less whatever-is-to-follow-Prague-rid-
      den;
The future would be more wonderful,
And less blood and thunderful,
And very much less Nazi,
And very much more hotsy-totsy.
What a pity then that so many knaves haven't troubled
      to study their part,
Because obviously they don't realize that they are only
      cowards at heart,
And golly, what can you do with a knave

When he doesn't realize that like a coward at heart he
    is supposed to behave?
Particularly when the knave seems to be a creature of
    whim,
And believes that if you have something he wants it is
    you who are the knave and therefore it is you who
    like all knaves are a coward at heart and not him?
I think that Mr. T. C. H. Jacobs has a splendid idea,
    but I also think it is up to him to make the start;
I think he should follow the arrantest knave he can
    find into a dark alley or a Polish corridor at mid-
    night and convince him first that he is a knave and
    second that he is a coward at heart,
And should he happily survive,
Why he can continue until he has convinced all other
    knaves alive,
And their too too solid hearts into knavish cowardice
    will melt,
And life will at last become truly heavenly and svelte.

FRAGONARD

There was an old miser named Clarence,
Who simonized both of his parents.
"The initial expense,"
He remarked, "is immense,
But I'll save it on wearance and tearance."

ELECTRA BECOMES MORBID

I

Abandon for a moment, friends,
Your frivolous means, your futile ends;
Life is not wholly beer and skittles,
A treasure hunt for love and victuals;
And so at times I think we ought
To pause and think a sobering thought.
Myself, I feel a dark despair
When I consider human hair.
I'm chicken-hearted, beetle-browed,
As I behold the heedless crowd,
Knowing each carefree individual
The slave of hair that runs on schidual.
On every human head or chin
It's falling out or growing in.
You whistling adolescent scholar,
Released from Ye Olde Tonsorial Parlor,
Runs up his neck with fingers tense
Like sticks along a picket fence.
His scalp is all Bay Rum and bristles,
Therefore he's pleased and therefore whistles.
Yea, he rejoices, quite unknowing
That all the time his hair is growing.
O woe is you, unhappy scholar,
Next month you'll be back in the tonsorial parlor.

II

Myself I feel a dark despair,
When I consider human hair,

(Fine filaments sprouting from the skin),
I tremble like an aspirin.
For men and women everywhere
Unconsciously are growing hair,
Or, if the other hand you choose,
With every breath a hair they lose.
Unbid it cometh, likewise goeth,
And oftentimes it's doing boeth.
This habit is the chief determinant
Why permanent waves are less than permanent.
You rise, Madame, you face your mirror,
You utter cries of shame and terror.
What though to males you look all right?
For heaven's sake, your hair's a sight.
You hasten to the Gallic lair
Where lurks Maurice, or Jean or Pierre.
Between arrival and departure
You suffer hours of vicious torture,
At last emerging, white and weak,
But sure at least your mane is chic.
Thus you rejoice, my dear, unknowing
That all the time your hair is growing.
The waves so dearly purchasèd
Next month will have grown a foot or so away from
    your head.

III

I've said, I think, I think we ought
To think at times a sobering thought.
Man's lot it is to be a field

For crops that no nutrition yield,
That filter through his tender skin
And ripen on his head or chin.
I face mankind and shudder, knowing
That everybody's hair is growing;
That lovers, linked in darkened hallways,
Are capped with hair that groweth always;
That millions, shaven in the morning,
At eve find beards their jowls adorning;
That hair is creeping through the scalps
Of yodelers yodeling in the Alps,
And pushing through the epidermises
Of peasants frolicking at kermises;
And poking bravely through the pores
Of cannibals on tropic shores;
That freezing, scorching, raining, snowing,
People's hair is always growing.
I contemplate with dark despair
The awful force of growing hair,
Although admitting, to be quite honest,
That it will be worth a million Niagaras to humanity if
    Science can ever get it harnessed.

REFLECTION ON A WICKED WORLD

Purity
Is obscurity.

I am now about to make a remark that I suppose most
    parents will think me hateful for,

Though as a matter of fact I am only commenting on
    a condition that they should be more than grateful
    for.

What I want to say is, that of luckiness it seems to me
    to be the height

That babies aren't very bright.

Now listen to me for a minute, all you proud progeni-
    tors who boast that your bedridden infant offspring
    of two months or so are already bright enough to
    get into Harvard or Stanford or Notre Dame or
    Fordham;

Don't you realize that the only thing that makes life
    at all bearable to those selfsame offspring is being
    rather backward, and that if they had any sense
    at all they would lose no time in perishing of
    boredom?

Good heavens, I can think of no catastrophe more im-
    mense

Than a baby with sense,

Because one thing at least, willy-nilly, you must believe,

And that is, that a baby has twenty-four hours a day to
    get through with just the same as we've.

Some people choose to wonder about virtue and others
    about crime,

But I choose to wonder how babies manage to pass the
time.
They can't pass it in tennis or badminton or golf,
Or in going around rescuing people from Indians and
then marrying somebody else the way Pocahontas
did with the Messrs. Smith and Rolfe;
They can't pass it in bridge or parchesi or backgammon,
Or in taking the subway to Wall Street and worship-
ping of Mammon;
How then do they manage to enthuse themselves,
And amuse themselves?
Well, partly they sleep,
And mostly they weep,
And the rest of the time they relax
On their backs,
And eat, by régime specifically, but by nature om-
nivorously,
And vocalize vocivorously.
That, to make it short,
Is about all they can do in the way of sport;
So whatever may come,
I am glad that babies are dumb.
I shudder to think what for entertainment they would
do
Were they as bright as me or you.

There is a knocking in the skull,
An endless silent shout
Of something beating on a wall,
And crying, Let me out.

That solitary prisoner
Will never hear reply,
No comrade in eternity
Can hear the frantic cry.

No heart can share the terror
That haunts his monstrous dark;
The light that filters through the chinks
No other eye can mark.

When flesh is linked with eager flesh,
And words run warm and full,
I think that he is loneliest then,
The captive in the skull.

Caught in a mesh of living veins,
In cell of padded bone,
He loneliest is when he pretends
That he is not alone.

We'd free the incarcerate race of man
That such a doom endures
Could only you unlock my skull,
Or I creep into yours.

The Murrays are hunting a house,
They are tired of living in flats.
They long for a personal mouse,
And a couple of personal cats.
They are hunting a house to inhabit,
An Eden, or even an Arden,
They are thinking of keeping a rabbit,
They are thinking of digging a garden.
How giddy the Murrays have grown,
To aspire to a house of their own!

Oh, hurry, hurry!
Says Mrs. Murray.
Tarry awhile, says he,
If you care for a house
As is a house,
You'd better leave it to me.
I'd like an orchard, apple or peach,
I'd like an accessible bathing beach,
And a den for unwinding detective plots,
And a lawn for practising mashie shots,
And open fires,
And a pleasant sunroom,
A handy garage,
And perhaps a gunroom,
And an atmosphere exempt of static,
And a furnace silent and automatic.
For such a house

I would hurry, hurry—
I'm a practical man,
Says Mr. Murray.

The Murrays of 17 B,
The Murrays are going away,
From the wireless in 17 C,
And the parties in 17 A.
For the Murrays are tired of flats,
They are rapidly growing aloof,
As they dream of their personal cats,
As they dream of their personal roof.
Their friends cannot smother their merriment
When they speak of the Murrays' experiment.

Oh, hurry, hurry!
Says Mr. Murray.
Tarry awhile, says she.
When we choose a house,
Let us choose a house
As nice as a house can be.
With a dozen windows South and East,
And a dozen capacious cupboards at least,
And a laundry lilting with light and air,
And a porch for a lady to dry her hair,
And plenty of sun,
And plenty of shade,
And a neat little place
For a neat little maid,

And a wall with roses clambering wild,
And a quiet room for a sleepy child.
If you happen to see it,
Hurry, hurry!
For that's the house,
Says Mrs. Murray.

THE RABBITS

Here's a verse about rabbits
That doesn't mention their habits.

The Murrays are snug in their house,
They are finished forever with flats;
They longed for a personal mouse,
And room to swing dozens of cats.
They longed for a hearth and a doorway,
In Arden, or maybe in Eden,
But the Eden is rather like Norway,
And the Arden like winter in Sweden.
How baffled the Murrays have grown
Since they live in a house of their own!

Oh hurry hurry!
Says Mrs. Murray.
But listen, my dear, says he,
If you want the house
A temperate house,
You'd better not leave it to me.
I've learned the knack of swinging a cat,
But I can't coerce the thermostat.
The furnace has given a gruesome cough,
And something has cut the fuel off,
And the heart of the nursery radiator
Is cold as the prose of Walter Pater,
And I've telephoned for the service men
But they can't get here until after ten,
So swaddle the children,
And hurry, hurry —
I'm a practical man,
Says Mr. Murray.

The Murrays are vague about fuses,
And mechanical matters like that,
And each of them frequently muses
On the days when they lived in a flat.
Was the plumbing reluctant to plumb?
Was the climate suggestive of Canada?
Did the radio crackle and hum?
You simply called down to the janada!
The Murrays have found no replacement
For the genius who lived in the basement.

Oh, hurry, hurry!
Says Mr. Murray.
I'm doing my best, says she,
But it's hard to scrub
In a tepid tub,
So the guests must wait for me;
And tell them they'll get their cocktails later
When you've managed to fix the refrigerator.
And explain if the coffee looks like water,
That the stove is as queer as a seventh daughter,
And I will be down as soon as able
To unstick the drawers of my dressing table.

There's a car at the door, says Mrs. Murray,
The doorbell's broken, so hurry, hurry!
Oh, I don't regret
Being wed to you,
But I wish I could wed
A janitor too.

Once there was a man and he wasn't famous for his
    clothes,
He was famous for his bon mots.
Dinner parties waited hungrily if he didn't come in
    till late
Because they could count on him to scintillate;
Just give him a cocktail or two to relax him
And you would be repaid with an epigram or a
    maxim;
He was invariably original,
And he did not have to depend for his effect on the
    indelicate or sacrileginal;
Of quips and anecdotes he was a warehouse,
And everybody wanted him at their house.
Yes indeed, he was quite a wit,
And then one day he suddenly quit.
He seldom went out and when he did go out he seldom
    opened his mouth,
And when he did, it was only to remark on the cur-
    rent blizzard or flood or drouth;
On scintillation he clamped down a total embargo,
And his most stimulating remark to a dinner partner in
    three months was, So you're from Louisville, I
    used to know some people named Perkins in
    Louisville, but it seems to me I heard they'd
    moved to Chicago.
And at first everybody was patient but at last their brows
    grew darkling,

And they went to him and said, Look here, how about
    a little sparkling?

And he said, Do you see these lips?

And they said they did, and he said, Well they shall
    never more be crossed by wanton wiles and cranks
    and quips.

He said, I have spent my life studying the fundamentals
    of wit and humor and table talk,

I have spent a fortune in time and effort to master the
    art of stimulating and able talk;

To every aphorism of mine you ever quoted,

Why, years of experience were devoted,

And then, he said, and then the baby is told to speak to
    Mr. Katz the grocer on the telephone, Go ahead,
    baby, speak to Mr. Katz, and the baby says Meow,

And the spasms of mirth raised by baby's repartee still
    echo in my ears right now.

No, he said, hereafter count me not a wit, count me
    simply a good neighbor.

I am too old and proud to compete with unskilled
    labor.

LOVE UNDER THE REPUBLICANS
(OR DEMOCRATS)

Come live with me and be my love
And we will all the pleasures prove
Of a marriage conducted with economy
In the Twentieth Century Anno Donomy.
We'll live in a dear little walk-up flat
With practically room to swing a cat
And a potted cactus to give it hauteur
And a bathtub equipped with dark brown water.
We'll eat, without undue discouragement
Foods low in cost but high in nouragement
And quaff with pleasure, while chatting wittily,
The peculiar wine of Little Italy.
We'll remind each other it's smart to be thrifty
And buy our clothes for something-fifty.
We'll stand in line on holidays
For seats at unpopular matinees,
And every Sunday we'll have a lark
And take a walk in Central Park.
And one of these days not too remote
I'll probably up and cut your throat.

There is something to be said for the Victorians

Even though they refused to believe they were descended from apes and saurians;

Because take their low opinion of exposure anatomical,

Why I have a feeling that they felt it was not so much immoral as just plain comical.

They realized that most people are big where they should be littler and little where they should be bigger,

And they would rather have had their bathing suit laughed at than their figure.

Yes they wore the costumes they did because they knew that they were not ancient Greeks,

And it is a moot question which is more ludicrous on the beach, the cloistered rompers of the Nineties, or today's ubiquitous physiques.

The belle of the Nineties tiptoeing down the steps of the bathing machine may have had the natural lines of a Langtry or again of a prize-winning pumpkin or of a homeless heifer after an extended drought,

But thanks to the marquee enswathing her she got the benefit of the doubt.

Whereas today at Miami or Coney or Catalina,

Why practically everyone is forced to face the fact that their beloved is built like either a flute or a concertina.

I have a theory about physiological disclosures along the strand;

I believe they account for Sally Rand;
I believe that when people have seen a certain number
　　of undraped figures like a concertina or a flute,
Well, finally they are willing to pay any amount just to
　　see a beaut,
So now it's a hot sultry day and you may all run down
　　to the beach for a swim and a look.
I'm going to put on Uncle Elmer's bathing suit and
　　sit in the tub and read a Victorian book.

REMINISCENT REFLECTION

When I consider how my life is spent,
I hardly ever repent.

Mr. and Mrs. F. X. Pleasants
Request the honor of my presence,
On Saturday the twenty-fourth,
To watch their daughter, Barbara North,
Succumb in holy matrimony
To Mr. Maximilian Coney.
A murrain on you, Mr. and Mrs. Pleasants!
I hope you turn into friends of Annie Besant's!

Bishop Apse will do the trick;
He's just the kind that mothers pick.
He has a noble velvet voice
That makes a mother's heart rejoice
And fills a mother's handkerchief
With briny evidence of grief.
A murrain on you too, old Bishop Apse!
I hope you get caught in some vicious moral lapse!

The ushers in their coats of black
Will lead old ladies forth and back,
While bridesmaids in their flowery frocks
Bloom round the bride like hollyhocks.
Who knows but what some sidelong glance
Will propagate a new romance?
A murrain on every bridesmaid and every usher!
I hope they all get spattered with oil from a gusher!

I'll wish some wishes for Mr. Coney
In honor of his matrimony.

I wish him moths, I wish him mice,
I wish him cocktails lacking ice.
I wish him a life abrupt and lonely,
I wish him a wife in title only.
A murrain, a murrain upon you, Maximilian!
If I wish you one death before evening I wish you a
    billion!

What have I left for Barbara North
Who changes her name on the twenty-fourth?
A hundred theater-ticket stubs,
Matches and corks from supper clubs,
A dozen notes whose theme is If,
Some lipstick on a handkerchief —
A lesser soul of spite would be a harborer;
Not I. No murrain at all upon you, Barbara!

DON'T CRY, DARLING, IT'S BLOOD
ALL RIGHT

Whenever poets want to give you the idea that some-
thing is particularly meek and mild,
They compare it to a child,
Thereby proving that though poets with poetry may be
rife
They don't know the facts of life.
If of compassion you desire either a tittle or a jot,
Don't try to get it from a tot.
Hard-boiled, sophisticated adults like me and you
May enjoy ourselves thoroughly with Little Women
and Winnie-the-Pooh,
But innocent infants these titles from their reading
course eliminate
As soon as they discover that it was honey and nuts
and mashed potatoes instead of human flesh that
Winnie-the-Pooh and Little Women ate.
Innocent infants have no use for fables about rabbits
or donkeys or tortoises or porpoises,
What they want is something with plenty of well-
mutilated corpoises.
Not on legends of how the rose came to be a rose instead of a petunia is their fancy fed,
But on the inside story of how somebody's bones got
ground up to make somebody else's bread.
They'll go to sleep listening to the story of the little
beggarmaid who got to be queen by being kind to
the bees and the birds,

But they're all eyes and ears the minute they suspect a
      wolf or a giant is going to tear some poor wood-
      cutter into quarters or thirds.
It really doesn't take much to fill their cup;
All they want is for somebody to be eaten up.
Therefore I say unto you, all you poets who are so crazy
      about meek and mild little children and their
      angelic air,
If you are sincere and really want to please them, why
      just go out and get yourselves devoured by a bear.

Candy
Is dandy
But liquor
Is quicker.

INVOCATION

("Smoot Plans Tariff Ban on Improper Books" — NEWS ITEM)

Senator Smoot (Republican, Ut.)
Is planning a ban on smut.
Oh root-ti-toot for Smoot of Ut.
And his reverent occiput.
Smite, Smoot, smite for Ut.,
Grit your molars and do your dut.,
Gird up your l—ns,
Smite h–p and th–gh,
We'll all be Kansas
By and by.

Smite, Smoot, for the Watch and Ward,
For Hiram Johnson and Henry Ford,
For Bishop Cannon and John D., Junior,
For Governor Pinchot of Pennsylvunia,
For John S. Sumner and Elder Hays
And possibly Edward L. Bernays,
For Orville Poland and Ella Boole,
For Mother Machree and the Shelton pool.
When smut's to be smitten
Smoot will smite
For G–d, for country,
And Fahrenheit.

Senator Smoot is an institute
Not to be bribed with pelf;
He guards our homes from erotic tomes
By reading them all himself.

Smite, Smoot, smite for Ut.,
They're smuggling smut from Balt. to Butte!
Strongest and sternest
Of your s–x
Scatter the scoundrels
From Can. to Mex.!

Smite, Smoot, for Smedley Butler,
For any good man by the name of Cutler,
Smite for the W.C.T.U.,
For Rockne's team and for Leader's crew,
For Florence Coolidge and Admiral Byrd,
For Billy Sunday and John D., Third,
For Grantland Rice and for Albie Booth,
For the Woman's Auxiliary of Duluth,
Smite, Smoot,
Be rugged and rough,
Smut if smitten
Is front-page stuff.

One human hellgramite that I think we could all dis-
 pense with
Is he who in every pleasant mixed gathering insists on
 dragging in the kind of anecdote that should, if
 employed, be employed only to entertain gents
 with.
As a rule, when he is among his fellow men he is meek
 as a mouse,
But just watch him when there are three or four ladies,
 preferably sensitive, in the house.
It is on such an occasion
That he elects to be most rabidly Rabelaisian.
His persiflage would embarrass
The late Frank Harris,
And as you watch him scintillating
You have an overwhelming conviction that the room
 needs vintilating.
It isn't that you yourself have never guffawed
At humor that is, to put it mildly, broad,
Or consider yourself too nice
To indulge once in a while in a bit of risquéting on
 thin ice;
It's just that under the circumstances the mildew that
 passes for wit with this weevil
Happens to throw your digestive system into a revulsive
 upheaval.
Sometimes he fancies himself as a Lothario,

And other times as the principal comedian of a side-
    splitting obscenario,
But if you chance to grow restive
As his quips and cranks and wanton wiles get continually
    more suggestive,
And venture the opinion that a trip to the laundry
Could hardly fail to benefit some of the double en-
    tendry,
He will retort that his intentions and his remarks are
    all irreproachably refined,
And that if you see something wrong about them it
    only proves conclusively that you have a vulgar
    mind.
So after that, everybody is on the spot
And nobody knows whether to laugh or not,
And the evening gets more and more uncomfortable
    and at the same time duller and duller
As every few minutes he trots out a horse of another
    off-color.
This I believe is his way of demonstrating that he is
    Sophisticated and not Provincial,
And if every good old sophisticated night-club pro-
    prietor and gangster on Broadway took him for a
    good old sophisticated ride I should consider it
    nothing less than Providintial.

MY DADDY

I have a funny daddy
Who goes in and out with me,
And everything that baby does
My daddy's sure to see,
And everything that baby says
My daddy's sure to tell.
You must have read my daddy's verse.
I hope he fries in hell.

WHEN YOU SAY THAT, SMILE!

or

ALL RIGHT THEN, DON'T SMILE

When the odds are long,
And the game goes wrong,
Does your joie de vivre diminish?
Have you little delight
In an uphill fight?
Do you wince at a Garrison finish?
Then here's my hand, my trusty partner!
I've always wanted a good disheartener.

Oh, things are frequently what they seem,
And this is wisdom's crown:
Only the game fish swims upstream,
But the sensible fish swims down.

Well, how is your pulse
When a cad insults
The lady you're cavaliering?
Are you willing to wait
To retaliate
Till the cad is out of hearing?
Then here's my hand, my trusty companion,
And may neither one of us fall in a canyon.

For things are frequently what they seem,
And this is wisdom's crown:
Only the game fish swims upstream,
But the sensible fish swims down.

There is a thought that I have tried not to but cannot
    help but think,
Which is, My goodness how much infants resemble
    people who have had too much to drink.
Tots and sots, so different and yet so identical!
What a humiliating coincidence for pride parental!
Yet when you see your little dumpling set sail across the
    nursery floor,
Can you conscientiously deny the resemblance to some-
    body who is leaving a tavern after having tried to
    leave it a dozen times and each time turned back
    for just one more?
Each step achieved
Is simply too good to be believed;
Foot somehow follows foot
And somehow manages to stay put;
Arms wildly semaphore,
Wild eyes seem to ask, Whatever did we get in such a
    dilemma for?
And their gait is more that of a duckling than a Greek
    goddessling or godling,
And in inebriates it's called staggering but in infants it's
    called toddling.
Another kinship with topers is also by infants exhibited,
Which is that they are completely uninhibited,
And they can't talk straight
Any more than they can walk straight;
Their pronunciation is awful

And their grammar is flawful,

And in adults it's drunken and maudlin and deplorable,

But in infants it's tunnin' and adorable.

So I hope you will agree that it is very hard to tell an infant from somebody who has gazed too long into the cup,

And really the only way you can tell them apart is to wait till next day, and the infant is the one that feels all right when it wakes up.

A LADY THINKS SHE IS THIRTY

Unwillingly Miranda wakes,
Feels the sun with terror,
One unwilling step she takes,
Shuddering to the mirror.

Miranda in Miranda's sight
Is old and gray and dirty;
Twenty-nine she was last night;
This morning she is thirty.

Shining like the morning star,
Like the twilight shining,
Haunted by a calendar,
Miranda sits a-pining.

Silly girl, silver girl,
Draw the mirror toward you;
Time who makes the years to whirl
Adorned as he adored you.

Time is timelessness for you;
Calendars for the human;
What's a year, or thirty, to
Loveliness made woman?

Oh, Night will not see thirty again,
Yet soft her wing, Miranda;
Pick up your glass and tell me, then —
How old is Spring, Miranda?

Torpor and sloth, torpor and sloth,
These are the cooks that unseason the broth.
Slothor and torp, slothor and torp
The directest of bee-line ambitions can warp.
He who is slothic, he who is torporal,
Will not be promoted to sergeant or corporal.
No torporer drowsy, no comatose slother
Will make a good banker, not even an author.
Torpor I deprecate, sloth I deplore,
Torpor is tedious, sloth is a bore.
Sloth is a bore, and torpor is tedious,
Fifty parts comatose, fifty tragedious.
How drear, on a planet redundant with woes,
That sloth is not slumber, nor torpor repose.
That the innocent joy of not getting things done
Simmers sulkily down to plain not having fun.
You smile in the morn like a bride in her bridalness
At the thought of a day of nothing but idleness.
By midday you're slipping, by evening a lunatic,
A perusing-the-newspapers-all-afternoonatic,
Worn to a wraith from the half-hourly jaunt
After glasses of water you didn't want,
And at last when onto your pallet you creep,
You discover yourself too tired to sleep.
O torpor and sloth, torpor and sloth,
These are the cooks that unseason the broth.
Torpor is harrowing, sloth it is irksome —
Everyone ready? Let's go out and worksome.

EDOUARD

A bugler named Dougal MacDougal
Found ingenious ways to be frugal.
He learned how to sneeze
In various keys,
Thus saving the price of a bugle.

Once there was a man named Jarvis Gravel who was
    just a man named Jarvis Gravel except for one
    thing:
He hated spring.
And this was because once a Communist had said Come
    on down to Union Square, it's May Day,
And Jarvis went, thinking he had said Come on down
    to Union Square, it's pay day.
So from then on anything at all vernal
Was to him strictly infernal.
When he saw the first crocus poke its head up
He'd get a shovel and dig the entire bed up,
And he bought a horse and galloped back and forth
Tipping off the worms when the first robin started
    North.
To love the way of a man with a maid in the moonlight
    was something he never learnt,
And he spent a lot of beautiful balmy evenings moving
    FRESH PAINT signs from park benches that were
    freshly painted to ones that weren't,
And when he finally did marry a girl who made his
    pulses quicken
It was merely because her name was Gale Winter-
    bottom and she was no spring chicken,
And one day during the worm-warning season he came
    home hungry after a hard day in the stirrup,
And she served him waffles and he objected to the
    May-pole syrup,

So she shot him through the heart, but his last words
    were ecstatic.
He said Thank you honey, it was thoughtful of you to
    use the autumnatic.

IN WHICH THE POET IS ASHAMED
BUT PLEASED

Of all the things that I would rather,
It is to be my daughter's father,
While she, with innocence divine,
Is quite contented to be mine.

I am distressingly aware
That this arrangement is unfair,
For I, when in my celibate garrison,
Acquired some standard of comparison.

I visited nurseries galore,
Compiled statistics by the score,
And gained experience from a crew
Of children passing in review.

And some were fair and some were dark
And some were clothed and some were stark,
And some were howling, teasing demons,
And some as sweet as Mrs. Hemans.

I saw the best that parents vaunted;
They weren't exactly what I wanted;
Yet, all the offspring that I faced,
They served to cultivate my taste.

Thus, let the miser praise the mintage,
And let the vintner praise the vintage;
I'm conscious that in praising her,
I'm speaking as a connoisseur.

While she, poor dear, has never known
A father other than her own.
She wots of other girls' papas
No more than of the Persian Shah's.

Within her head no notion stirs
That some are better men than hers;
That some are richer, some are kinder,
Some are solider, some refineder,

That some are vastly more amusing
Some fitter subjects for enthusing,
That some are cleverer, some are braver,
Than the one that fortune gave her.

What fortune set us side by side,
Her scope so narrow, mine so wide?
We owe to this sweet dispensation
Our mutual appreciation.

FUNEBRIAL REFLECTION

Among the anthropophagi
People's friends are people's sarcophagi.

You don't need to study any ponderous tome
To find out how to make your out-of-town guests feel
not at home,
Because there is one way which couldn't be exquisiter
For enthralling the visitor.
You plan a little gathering informal and sociable
And you ask a few friends whose manners are irre-
proaciable,
And you speak up with all the pride of Mr. Dewey an-
nouncing a couple of important impending arrests,
And you say Friends, this is Mr. and Mrs. Comfit-
monger, my out-of-town guests,
And you even amplify your introduction so as to break
the ice with more velocity,
And you tell them that Mrs. Comfitmonger used to be
a policewoman and Mr. Comfitmonger is a piano
tuner of no mean virtuosity,
And you hint that Mr. Comfitmonger has had some
pretty intriguing experiences in his years as a vir-
tuoso,
And that Mrs. Comfitmonger while pounding her beat
has dealt with personalities who would scare the
pants off Lombroso,
And that everything is all set for a dandy evening of
general chitchat is what you think,
And you retire to the pantry to prepare everybody a
drink,
And you hear the brouhaha of vivacious voices,

And your heart rejoices,

Because it seems that your friends find Mr. Comfit-monger's anecdotes of life under the Steinways fascinating,

And are spellbound by Mrs. Comfitmonger's articulate opposition to arson and assassinating,

And you say This party is indeed de luxe,

And you emerge to find all your friends excitedly discussing putts that wouldn't go down and stocks that wouldn't go up, and Mr. and Mrs. Comfitmonger over in a corner leafing through your books,

And if you think you can turn the conversation to Palestrina or police work,

You've taken on a mighty pretty job of piecework,

Because if there is one thing in which everybody's home-team friends are unerring,

It is to confine their conversation to mutual acquaintances and episodes as to which your visiting friends have no idea of to what they are referring.

Most people are only vocal
When talking local.

This is the day, this is the day!
I knew as soon as the sun's first ray
Crept through the slats of the cot,
And opened the eyes of a tot,
And the tot would rather have slept,
And, therefore, wept.
This is the day that is wrong,
The day when the only song
Is a skirling lamentation
Of continuous indignation,
When the visage is ireful,
The voice, direful,
And the early, pearly teeth
Snick like a sword in the sheath,
When the fists are clenched,
And the cheeks are drenched
In full-fed freshets and tumbling, tumultuous tor-
    rents
Of virtuous abhorrence,
When loud as the challenging trumpets of John at
    Lepanto
Rings the clarion, "I don't want to."
This is the day, the season,
Of wrongs without reason,
The day when the prunes and the cereal
Taste like building material,
When the spinach tastes only like spinach, and honey
    and sugar

Raise howls like the yowls of a quarrelsome puma or
    cougar,
When the wail is not to be hushed
Nor the hair to be brushed,
When life is frustration, and either
A person must be all alone or have somebody with her,
    and tolerates neither,
When outdoors is worse than in, and indoors than out,
    and both too dull to be borne,
And dolls are flung under the bed and books are torn,
When people humiliate a person
With their clumsily tactful attempts to conciliate a
    person,
When music no charm possesses,
Nor hats, nor mittens, nor dresses,
When the frowning fortress is woe
And the watchword is No.
You owners of children who pass this day with for-
    bearance,
You indeed are parents!

THE CANARY

The song of canaries
Never varies,
And when they're moulting
They're pretty revolting.

People who have what they want are very fond of telling
    people who haven't what they want that they really
    don't want it,
And I wish I could afford to gather all such people into
    a gloomy castle on the Danube and hire half a
    dozen capable Draculas to haunt it.
I don't mind their having a lot of money, and I don't
    care how they employ it,
But I do think that they damn well ought to admit
    they enjoy it.
But no, they insist on being stealthy
About the pleasures of being wealthy,
And the possession of a handsome annuity
Makes them think that to say how hard it is to make
    both ends meet is their bounden duity.
You cannot conceive of an occasion
Which will find them without some suitable evasion.
Yes indeed, with arguments they are very fecund;
Their first point is that money isn't everything, and
    that they have no money anyhow is their second.
Some people's money is merited,
And other people's is inherited,
But wherever it comes from,
They talk about it as if it were something you got pink
    gums from.
This may well be,
But if so, why do they not relieve themselves of the
    burden by transferring it to the deserving poor or
    to me?

Perhaps indeed the possession of wealth is constantly
    distressing,
But I should be quite willing to assume every curse of
    wealth if I could at the same time assume every
    blessing.
The only incurable troubles of the rich are the troubles
    that money can't cure,
Which is a kind of trouble that is even more trouble-
    some if you are poor.
Certainly there are lots of things in life that money
    won't buy, but it's very funny —
Have you ever tried to buy them without money?

THE TALE OF CUSTARD THE DRAGON

Belinda lived in a little white house,
With a little black kitten and a little gray mouse,
And a little yellow dog and a little red wagon,
And a realio, trulio, little pet dragon.

Now the name of the little black kitten was Ink,
And the little gray mouse, she called her Blink,
And the little yellow dog was sharp as Mustard,
But the dragon was a coward, and she called him
    Custard.

Custard the dragon had big sharp teeth,
And spikes on top of him and scales underneath,
Mouth like a fireplace, chimney for a nose,
And realio, trulio daggers on his toes.

Belinda was as brave as a barrel full of bears,
And Ink and Blink chased lions down the stairs,
Mustard was as brave as a tiger in a rage,
But Custard cried for a nice safe cage.

Belinda tickled him, she tickled him unmerciful,
Ink, Blink and Mustard, they rudely called him Per-
    cival,
They all sat laughing in the little red wagon
At the realio, trulio, cowardly dragon.

Belinda giggled till she shook the house,
And Blink said Weeck! which is giggling for a mouse,

Ink and Mustard rudely asked his age,
When Custard cried for a nice safe cage.

Suddenly, suddenly they heard a nasty sound,
And Mustard growled, and they all looked around,
Meowch! cried Ink, and Ooh! cried Belinda,
For there was a pirate, climbing in the winda.

Pistol in his left hand, pistol in his right,
And he held in his teeth a cutlass bright,
His beard was black, one leg was wood;
It was clear that the pirate meant no good.

Belinda paled, and she cried Help! Help!
But Mustard fled with a terrified yelp,
Ink trickled down to the bottom of the household
And little mouse Blink strategically mouseholed.

But up jumped Custard, snorting like an engine,
Clashed his tail like irons in a dungeon,
With a clatter and a clank and a jangling squirm
He went at the pirate like a robin at a worm.

The pirate gaped at Belinda's dragon,
And gulped some grog from his pocket flagon,
He fired two bullets, but they didn't hit,
And Custard gobbled him, every bit.

Belinda embraced him, Mustard licked him,
No one mourned for his pirate victim.

Ink and Blink in glee did gyrate
Around the dragon that ate the pyrate.

Belinda still lives in her little white house,
With her little black kitten and her little gray mouse,
And her little yellow dog and her little red wagon,
And her realio, trulio, little pet dragon.

Belinda is as brave as a barrel full of bears,
And Ink and Blink chase lions down the stairs,
Mustard is as brave as a tiger in a rage,
But Custard keeps crying for a nice safe cage.

POLITICAL REFLECTION

*Like an art-lover looking at the Mona Lisa in the Louvre
Is the New York Herald Tribune looking at Mr.
Herbert Houvre.*

I do not like the winter wind
That whistles from the North.
My upper teeth and those beneath,
They jitter back and forth.
Oh, some are hanged, and some are skinned,
And others face the winter wind.

I do not like the summer sun
That scorches the horizon.
Though some delight in Fahrenheit,
To me it's deadly pizen.
I think that life would be more fun
Without the simmering summer sun.

I do not like the signs of spring,
The fever and the chills,
The icy mud, the puny bud,
The frozen daffodils.
Let other poets gayly sing;
I do not like the signs of spring.

I do not like the foggy fall
That strips the maples bare;
The radiator's mating call,
The dank, rheumatic air.
I fear that taken all in all,
I do not like the foggy fall.

The winter sun is always kind,
And summer wind's a savior,
And I'll merrily sing of fall and spring
When they're on their good behavior.
But otherwise I see no reason
To speak in praise of any season.

What am I doing, daughter mine?
A-haying while the sun doth shine;
Gathering rosebuds while I may
To hoard against a barren day;
Reveling in the brief sensation
Of basking in your admiration.
Oh, now, when you are almost five
I am the lordliest man alive;
Your gaze is blind to any flaw,
And brimming with respect and awe.
You think me handsome, strong and brave,
You come at morn to watch me shave.
The neighbors' insults lose their sting
When you encourage me to sing,
And like a fashion plate I pose
While you compliment my clothes.
Who wishes his self-esteem to thrive
Should belong to a girl of almost five.
But almost five can't last forever,
And wide-eyed girls grow tall and clever.
Few creatures others less admire
Than a lass of seventeen her sire.
What humiliation must you weather
When we are seen in public together!
Perchance I'll munch a stick of gum,
Or in the theater brazenly hum;
My hat, I'm sure, will flout the law
Laid down for hats at Old Nassau;

My anecdotes you'll strive to stanch,
And at my table manners blanch;
My every word and every deed
Will agony and embarrassment breed;
Your goal of goals, the end of your ends,
To hide me forever from your friends.
Therefore I now chant roundelays,
And rollick in your pride and praise;
Too soon the nymph that you will be
Will shudder when she looks at me.

ARTHUR

There was an old man of Calcutta,
Who coated his tonsils with butta,
Thus converting his snore
From a thunderous roar
To a soft, oleaginous mutta.

MA, WHAT'S A BANKER?

or

HUSH, MY CHILD

The North wind doth blow,
And we shall have snow,
And what will the banker do then, poor thing?
Will he go to the barn
To keep himself warm,
And hide his head under his wing?
Is he on the spot, poor thing, poor thing?
Probably not, poor thing.

For when he is good,
He is not very good,
And when he is bad he is horrider,
And the chances are fair
He is taking the air
Beside a cabaña in Florida.
But the wailing investor, mean thing, mean thing,
Disturbs his siesta, poor thing.

He will plunge in the pool,
But he makes it a rule
To plunge with his kith and his kin,
And whisper about
That it's time to get out
When the widows and orphans get in.
He only got out, poor thing, poor thing,
Yet they call him a tout, poor thing.

His heart simply melts
For everyone else;
By love and compassion he's ridden;
The pay of his clerks
To reduce, how it irks!
But he couldn't go South if he didden.
I'm glad there's a drink within reach, poor thing,
As he weeps on the beach, poor thing.

May he someday find peace
In a temple in Greece,
Where the Government harbors no rancor;
May Athens and Sparta
Play host to the martyr,
And purchase a bond from the banker.
With the banker in Greece, poor thing, poor thing,
We can cling to our fleece, Hot Cha!

How does a person get to be a capable liar?

That is something that I respectfully inquiar,

Because I don't believe a person will ever set the world
on fire

Unless they are a capable lire.

Some wise man said that words were given to us to
conceal our thoughts,

But if a person has nothing but truthful words why
their thoughts haven't even the protection of a
pair of panties or shoughts,

And a naked thought is ineffectual as well as improper,

And hasn't a chance in the presence of a glib chinchilla-
clad whopper.

One of the greatest abilities a person can have, I guess,

Is the ability to say Yes when they mean No and No
when they mean Yes.

Oh to be Machiavellian, oh to be unscrupulous, oh, to
be glib!

Oh to be ever prepared with a plausible fib!

Because then a dinner engagement or a contract or a
treaty is no longer a fetter,

Because liars can just logically lie their way out of it if
they don't like it or if one comes along that they
like better;

And do you think their conscience prickles?

No, it tickles.

And please believe that I mean every one of these lines
as I am writing them

Because once there was a small boy who was sent to the
    drugstore to buy some bitter stuff to put on his
    nails to keep him from biting them,
And in his humiliation he tried to lie to the clerk
And it didn't work,
Because he said My mother sent me to buy some bit-
    ter stuff for a friend of mine's nails that bites them,
    and the clerk smiled wisely and said I wonder who
    that friend could be,
And the small boy broke down and said Me,
And it was me, or at least I was him,
And all my subsequent attempts at subterfuge have
    been equally grim,
And that is why I admire a suave prevarication because
    I prevaricate so awkwardly and gauchely,
And that is why I can never amount to anything po-
    litically or socially.

THE CAMEL

The camel has a single hump;
The dromedary, two;
Or else the other way around.
I'm never sure. Are you?

There is a town within a town,
Where my true love walks alone,
And green, oh, meadow green, is her gown,
And daffodil gold her shoon.

Unto that silent, secret place,
No street, no alley, leads.
A town without a market place,
No huckster crowd it feeds.

The wagon wheels without the wall,
They are not heard within.
The angry bells that clash and call,
They may not enter in.

And thunderheads their thunder lose;
Such is the stillness there,
That in the grassy avenues
The deer feeds, and the hare.

And there the hot sun softlier sifts,
And the harsh wind softlier blows,
And the frost melts, and the fog lifts,
And earlier springs the rose.

Within that town a lady walks
In dear serenity,
And lilies on their slender stalks
Less stately are than she.

Less delicate the violets are,
Less light of foot the deer,
Less lovely is the evening star,
Than she who walketh here.

I built that greedy outer town,
And she the town within.
When my own creature howls me down,
She bids me enter in.

Oh meadow, meadow green is her gown,
And daffodil gold her shoon.
God keep the town within a town,
Where my true love walks alone.

These here are words of radical advice for a young
  man looking for a job;
Young man, be a snob.
Yes, if you are in search of arguments against starting
  at the bottom,
Why I've gottom.
Let the personnel managers differ;
It's obvious that you will get on faster at the top than
  at the bottom because there are more people at the
  bottom than at the top so naturally the competi-
  tion at the bottom is stiffer.
If you need any further proof that my theory works,
Well, nobody can deny that presidents get paid more
  than vice-presidents and vice-presidents get paid
  more than clerks.
Stop looking at me quizzically;
I want to add that you will never achieve fortune in a
  job that makes you uncomfortable physically.
When anybody tells you that hard jobs are better for
  you than soft jobs be sure to repeat this text to
  them,
Postmen tramp around all day through rain and snow
  just to deliver people in cozy air-conditioned offices
  checks to them.
You don't need to interpret tea leaves stuck in a cup
To understand that people who work sitting down get
  paid more than people who work standing up.

Another thing about having a comfortable job is you
    not only accumulate more treasure;
You get more leisure.
So that when you find you have worked so comfortably
    that your waistline is a menace,
You correct it with golf or tennis.
Whereas if in an uncomfortable job like piano-moving
    or stevedoring you indulge,
You have no time for exercise, you just continue to
    bulge.
To sum it up, young man, there is every reason to refuse
    a job that will make heavy demands on you cor-
    porally or manually,
And the only intelligent way to start your career is to
    accept a sitting position paying at least twenty-five
    thousand dollars annually.

THE ROOSTER

The rooster has a soul more bellicose
Than all your Ludendorffs and Jellicoes.
His step is prouder than Davy Crockett's,
As he swaggers by with his hands in his pockets.

How pleasant to sit on the beach,
On the beach, on the sand, in the sun,
With ocean galore within reach,
And nothing at all to be done!
No letters to answer,
No bills to be burned,
No work to be shirked,
No cash to be earned.
It is pleasant to sit on the beach
With nothing at all to be done.

How pleasant to look at the ocean,
Democratic and damp; indiscriminate;
It fills me with noble emotion
To think I am able to swim in it.
To lave in the wave,
Majestic and chilly,
Tomorrow I crave;
But today it is silly.
It is pleasant to look at the ocean;
Tomorrow, perhaps, I shall swim in it.

How pleasant to gaze at the sailors,
As their sailboats they manfully sail
With the vigor of vikings and whalers
In the days of the viking and whale.
They sport on the brink
Of the shad and the shark;

If it's windy they sink;
If it isn't, they park.
It is pleasant to gaze at the sailors,
To gaze without having to sail.

How pleasant the salt anaesthetic
Of the air and the sand and the sun;
Leave the earth to the strong and athletic,
And the sea to adventure upon.
But the sun and the sand
No contractor can copy;
We lie in the land
Of the lotus and poppy;
We vegetate, calm and aesthetic,
On the beach, on the sand, in the sun.

MR. PEACHEY'S PREDICAMENT

NO MOT PARADES

Once there was a man named Mr. Peachey and he
    lived on Park Avenue and played the harp and was
    an eligible bachelor but his social life was hapless,
And he thought at first it was because his parents came
    from Indianapless,
But one day he awoke from a troubled nap,
And said I am tired of this hapless social life, what I
    want is a social life simply teeming with hap.
It can't be, he said, that I don't play the harp enough,
I wonder if just possibly my wits are not sharp enough.
I know that I'm pretty noted
But I've never been quoted;
Perhaps the solution for me
Is some iridescent repartee;
Suppose before I next dine out I compose a series of
    epigrams of searing astringency
And then I shall be ready with a quip for any con-
    versational contingency.
So he composed a series of epigrams of indubitable
    variety,
And went to dine with some people way up in society.
And in the taxi he memorized his lines and held a
    solo rehearsal,
And he was delighted, because he said some people's
    humor is specialized but mine is universal.
There may well be a Mr. Shoemaker there who has

divorced a beautiful rich virtuous wife for a debt-
ridden hideous wife with a past,
And I'll say Shoemaker you should have stuck to your
last;
And suppose somebody remarks that the hostess looks
like a Titian I bring them up short,
I can answer, Looks like a Titian, eh? Do you mean
beaut- or mort-?
And I'll go right on and say While we're on the subject
of waltzes I'd like to play a little Haydn for you,
and I'll go to the piano and grope at the keys and
then look up impishly and speak,
And say I really don't know whether I'm playing Haydn
or Haydn seek.
Then after the laughter has died down I shall approach
some Yale man who has just returned from abroad
whom I wish to embarrass
And I'll ask him how he enjoyed the Boola-Boolavards
of Paris.
Oh, said Mr. Peachey gleefully, the days of my hapless
social life are over, I cannot help but be a wow,
I wish I was at the party right now.
But when he got to the party his hostess, who didn't
look like a Titian at all, she looked like a Dali, was
quite sharp,
And sent him right back to his Park Avenue apartment
to get his harp,
And today he is living in the old family mansion in
Indianapless
Where I'm sorry to say his social life is just as hapless.

THE SEA-GULL

Hark to the whimper of the sea-gull;
He weeps because he's not an ea-gull.
Suppose you were, you silly sea-gull,
Could you explain it to your she-gull?

Linell is clad in a gown of green,
She walks in state like a fairy queen.
Her train is tucked in a winsome bunch
Directly behind her royal lunch.
With a dignified skip and a haughty hop
Her golden slippers go clippety-clop.
I think I am Mummy, says Linell.
I'm Mummy too, says Isabel.

Linell has discovered a filmy veil;
The very thing for a swishy tail.
The waves wash over the nursery floor
And break on the rug with a rumbling roar;
The swishy tail gives a swishy swish;
She's off and away like a frightened fish.
Now I'm a mermaid, says Linell.
I'm mermaid too, says Isabel.

Her trousers are blue, her hair is kinky,
Her jacket is red and her skin is inky.
She is hiding behind a green umbrella;
She couldn't be Alice, or Cinderella,
Or Puss in Boots, or the Fiddlers Three;
Goodness gracious, who can she be?
I'm Little Black Sambo, says Linell.
I'm Sambo, too, says Isabel.

Clack the shutters. The blinds are drawn.
Click the switch, and the lights are gone.

Linell is under the blankets deep,
Murmuring down the hill to sleep.
Oh, deep in the soft and gentle dark
She stirs and chirps like a drowsy lark.
I love you, Mummy, says Linell.
Love Mummy too, says Isabel.

Noises new to sea and land
Issue from the circus band.
Each musician looks like mumps
From blowing umpah umpah umps.

Lovely girls in spangled pants
Ride on gilded elephants.
Elephants are useful friends,
They have handles on both ends;
They hold each other's hindmost handles
And flee from mice and Roman candles.
Their hearts are gold, their hides are emery,
And they have a most tenacious memory.

Notice also, girls and boys,
The circus horses' avoirdupois.
Far and wide the wily scouts
Seek these snow-white stylish stouts.
Calmer steeds were never found
Unattached to a merry-go-round.
Equestriennes prefer to jump
Onto horses pillow-plump.

Equestriennes will never ride
As other people do, astride.
They like to balance on one foot,
And wherever they get, they won't stay put.
They utter frequent whoops and yips,
And have the most amazing hips.

Pink seems to be their favorite color,
And very few things are very much duller.

Yet I for one am more than willing
That everything should be less thrilling.
My heart and lungs both bound and balk
When high-wire walkers start to walk.
They ought to perish, yet they don't;
Some fear they will, some fear they won't.

I lack the adjectives, verbs and nouns
To do full justice to the clowns.
Their hearts are constantly breaking, I hear,
And who am I to interfere?
I'd rather shake hands with Mr. Ringling
And tell him his circus is a beautiful thingling.

DRUSILLA

There was an old man of Schoharie
Who settled himself in a quarry.
And those who asked why
Got the candid reply,
"Today is the day of the soirée."

A GOOD PARENT'S GARDEN OF VISION

PART I: THE DREAM

In my bachelor days, no parent I,
My spirits fell as the weeks ran by,
And, tossing on my pallet, I dolefully thought
Of Time, the tri-motored Juggernaut,
Or paused at whiles amid my gardening
To listen for the sound of my arteries hardening.
But now I eagerly listen for
Senility knocking at the door.
You ask, and properly ask, no doubt,
Whence this astonishing right-about?
Why now so Frances Hodgson Bùrnett-y? —
Not Pelmanism, but paternity.
Come dotage, envelop me in your arms,
Old age, I ween, has its special charms.
I'll camp awhile by Jordan's water
And enjoy being a nuisance to my daughter.
The loving offspring of Mr. N.
Won't trouble her head with raw young men,
Young men who cry she is lissome and flowery,
Young men who inquire about her dowery.
She'll make young men all keep their distances,
She'll listen to her father's reministances,
She'll fondly lay out his favorite slippers,
And when he wears arctics she'll zip his zippers,
She'll nogg his eggs and she'll toast his kippers,
And disparage the quips of the current quippers.
She'll light his pipe and she'll mix his drinks

And conceal from her father every thought she thinks,
And he in his way and she in hern
Will be merry as a melody by Mr. Kern.

And he in his way and she in hern
Will be merry as ashes in a funeral urn.
She'll discourage his pipe and she'll hide his drinks,
And she'll tell her father every thought she thinks.
She'll make audible comments on his taste in togs,
She'll put his eggs in custards and not in noggs,
She'll object to the odor of kippering kippers,
She will laugh Ha Ha! at the current quippers,
She will leave the room when he dons his slippers,
When his buttons unbutton she will advocate zippers.
She'll see that parents keep their proper distances,
And she'll give young men a lot of reministances,
She'll look at her father like a beetle from the Bowery,
And ask why she hasn't a decent dowery,
And the only moments she'll be really merry
Will be pricing plots at the cemetery,
And I fear by the time his epitaph's read,
She'll be either a spinster or five times wed.

O pleasing daughter of Mr. N.,
His forebodings are happily beyond your ken,
And I gravely doubt that his querulous words
Retard the digestion of your whey and curds,
For children all choose their own sweet way —

Say Disobey, and they Datobey.
It's not that they're all in the pay of Belial,
It's only their way of being filial.
Some grow up hideous, others beautiful,
Some ungrateful and others dutiful;
Why try to prognosticate which yours will be?
There's nothing to do but wait and see.
Only nasty parents lose their nerve
At the prospect of getting what they deserve.
With a conscience as clear as mountain water
I await the best from my loving daughter.

LITERARY REFLECTION

Philo Vance
Needs a kick in the pance.

TWO AND ONE ARE A PROBLEM

Dear Miss Dix, I am a young man of half-past thirty-
 seven.

My friends say I am not unattractive, though to be
 kind and true is what I have always striven.

I am open-minded about beverages so long as they are
 grape, brandy or malt,

And I am generous to practically any fault.

Well Miss Dix not to beat around the bush, there is a
 certain someone who thinks I am pretty nice,

And I turn to you for advice.

You see, it started when I was away on the road

And returned to find a pair of lovebirds had taken up
 their residence in my abode.

Well I am not crazy about lovebirds, but I must say
 they looked very sweet in their gilded cage,

And their friendship had reached an advanced stage,

And I had just forgiven her who of the feathered
 fiancés was the donor of

When the houseboy caught a lost lovebird in the yard
 that we couldn't locate the owner of.

So then we had three, and it was no time for flippancy,

Because everybody knows that a lovebird without its
 own lovebird to love will pine away and die of the
 discrepancy,

So we bought a fourth lovebird for the third lovebird
 and they sat around very cozily beak to beak

And then the third lovebird that we had provided the

fourth lovebird for to keep it from dying died at
the end of the week,
So we were left with an odd lovebird and it was no time
for flippancy,
Because a lovebird without its own lovebird to love
will pine away and die of the discrepancy,
So we had to buy a fifth lovebird to console the fourth
lovebird that we had bought to keep the third
lovebird contented,
And now the fourth lovebird has lost its appetite, and
Miss Dix, I am going demented.
I don't want to break any hearts, but I got to know
where I'm at;
Must I keep on buying lovebirds, Miss Dix, or do you
think it would be all right to buy a cat?

What shall I do with So-and-So?
She won't say Yes and she won't say No.
She tiptoes around the cunningest traps
With a smile and a murmur of Perhaps.
At nine I'm Darling, at ten I'm You —
Tell me, what is a man to do
When the lady his life is based upon
Likes to be wooed but won't be won?

What shall I do with So-and-So?
She won't say Come and she won't say Go.
I'm on my way, but I don't know where —
I wouldn't care, if I didn't care.
Damn the man who invented the story
That a little suspense is salutory.
I swear, by lipstick and powder puff,
Fun is fun, but enough's enough!

What shall I do with So-and-So?
She confesses that I am her favorite beau;
But let the topic of marriage arise
And see the astonishment in her eyes!
Why am I chosen so to be harried?
Other people have gotten married.
Is every courtship conducted thus
Or is it only confined to us?

What shall I do with So-and-So?
If it isn't Yes it must be No,

But who so apathetic as me
To all the other fish in the sea?
On the other hand there's the other guess —
If it isn't No it must be Yes.
But just to be safe, love, I implore you
To let me give me your answer for you.

SONG OF THE OPEN ROAD

I think that I shall never see
A billboard lovely as a tree.
Indeed, unless the billboards fall
I'll never see a tree at all.

Listen to me, angel tot,
Whom I love an awful lot,
It will save a barrel of bother
If we understand each other.

Every time that I'm your herder
You think you get away with murder.
All right, infant, so you do,
But only because I want you to.

Baby's muscles are prodigious,
Baby's beautiful, not higious,
She can talk and walk and run
Like a daughter of a gun.

Well, you may be a genius, child,
And I a parent dull and mild;
In spite of which, and nevertheless,
I could lick you yet, I guess.

Forgive me, pet, if I am frank,
But truth is money in the bank;
I wish you to admire and love yourself,
But not to get too far above yourself.

When we race, you always win;
Baby, think before you grin.
It may occur to you, perhaps,
That Daddy's running under wraps.

When you hide behind the chair
And Daddy seeks you everywhere,
Behind the door, beneath the bed —
That's Daddy's heart, not Baby's head.

When I praise your speech in glee
And claim you talk as well as me,
That's the spirit, not the letter.
I know more words, and say them better.

In future, then, when I'm your herder,
Continue getting away with murder;
But know from him who murder endures,
It's his idea much more than yours.

Some singers sing of ladies' eyes,
And some of ladies' lips,
Refined ones praise their ladylike ways,
And coarse ones hymn their hips.
The Oxford Book of English Verse
Is lush with lyrics tender;
A poet, I guess, is more or less
Preoccupied with gender.
Yet I, though custom call me crude,
Prefer to sing in praise of food.

Food,
Yes, food,
Just any old kind of food.
Pooh for the cook,
And pooh for the price!
Some of it's nicer but all of it's nice.
Pheasant is pleasant, of course,
And terrapin, too, is tasty,
Lobster I freely endorse,
In pâté or patty or pasty.
But there's nothing the matter with butter,
And nothing the matter with jam,
And the warmest of greetings I utter
To the ham and the yam and the clam.
For they're food,
All food,
And I think very highly of food.

Though I'm broody at times
When bothered by rhymes,
I brood
On food.

Some painters paint the sapphire sea,
And some the gathering storm.
Others portray young lambs at play,
But most, the female form.
'Twas trite in that primeval dawn
When painting got its start,
That a lady with her garments on
Is Life, but is she Art?
By undraped nymphs
I am not wooed;
I'd rather painters painted food.

Food,
Just food,
Just any old kind of food.
Let it be sour
Or let it be sweet,
As long as you're sure it is something to eat.
Go purloin a sirloin, my pet,
If you'd win a devotion incredible;
And asparagus tips vinaigrette,
Or anything else that is edible.
Bring salad or sausage or scrapple,
A berry or even a beet.
Bring an oyster, an egg, or an apple,

As long as it's something to eat.
If it's food,
It's food;
Never mind what kind of food.
When I ponder my mind
I consistently find
It is glued
On food.

THE DUCK

Behold the duck.
It does not cluck.
A cluck it lacks.
It quacks.
It is specially fond
Of a puddle or pond.
When it dines or sups,
It bottoms ups.

Once there was a man named Mr. Artesian and his
    activity was tremendous,
And he grudged every minute away from his desk be-
    cause the importance of his work was so stupen-
    dous;
And he had one object all sublime,
Which was to save simply oodles of time.
He figured that sleeping eight hours a night meant that
    if he lived to be seventy-five he would have spent
    twenty-five years not at his desk but in bed,
So he cut his slumber to six hours which meant he only
    lost eighteen years and nine months instead,
And he figured that taking ten minutes for breakfast
    and twenty minutes for luncheon and half an hour
    for dinner meant that he spent three years, two
    months and fifteen days at the table,
So that by subsisting solely on bouillon cubes which he
    swallowed at his desk to save this entire period he
    was able,
And he figured that at ten minutes a day he spent a
    little over six months and ten days shaving,
So he grew a beard, which gave him a considerable
    saving,
And you might think that now he might have been
    satisfied, but no, he wore a thoughtful frown,
Because he figured that at two minutes a day he would
    spend thirty-eight days and a few minutes in ele-
    vators just traveling up and down,

So as a final timesaving device he stepped out the window of his office, which happened to be on the fiftieth floor,

And one of his partners asked "Has he vertigo?" and the other glanced out and down and said "Oh no, only about ten feet more."

Dear parents, I write you this letter
Because I thought I'd better;
Because I would like to know
Exactly which way to grow.

My milk I will leave undrunk
If you'd rather have me shrunk,
If your love it will further kindle,
I'll do my best to dwindle;

Or, on the other hand,
Do you wish me to expand?
I'll stuff like a greedy rajah
If you really want me larger.

All that I ask of you
Is to tell me which to do;
To whisper in accents mild
The proper size for a child.

I get so very confused
By the chidings commonly used.
Am I really such a dunce
As to err two ways at once?

When one mood you are in,
My bigness is a sin:
"Oh what a thing to do
For a great big girl like you!"

But then another time
Smallness is my crime:
"Stop doing whatever you're at;
You're far too little for that!"

Kind parents, be so kind
As to kindly make up your mind
And whisper in accents mild
The proper size for a child.

THE LAMA

The one-l lama,
He's a priest.
The two-l llama,
He's a beast.
And I will bet
A silk pajama
There isn't any
Three-l lllama.*

* The author's attention has been called to a type of con-
flagration known as a three-alarmer. Pooh.

GOODY FOR OUR SIDE AND YOUR
SIDE TOO

Foreigners are people somewhere else,
Natives are people at home;
If the place you're at is your habitat,
You're a foreigner, say in Rome.
But the scales of Justice balance true,
And tit only leads to tat,
So the man who's at home when he stays in Rome
Is abroad when he's where you're at.

When we leave the limits of the land in which
Our birth certificates sat us,
It does not mean just a change of scene,
But also a change of status.
The Frenchman with his fetching beard,
The Scot with his kilt and sporran,
One moment he may a native be,
And the next may find him foreign.

There's many a difference quickly found
Between the different races,
But the only essential differential
Is living in different places.
Yet such is the pride of prideful man,
From Austrians to Australians,
That wherever he is, he regards as his,
And the natives there, as aliens.

Oh, I'll be friends if you'll be friends,
The foreigner tells the native,
And we'll work together for our common ends
Like a preposition and a dative.
If our common ends seem mostly mine,
Why not, you ignorant foreigner?
And the native replies contrariwise;
And hence, my dears, the coroner.

So mind your manners when a native, please,
And doubly when you're not,
And Vickers and Krupp will soon fold up,
And Sopwith pawn his yacht.
One simple thought, if you have it pat,
Will eliminate the coroner:
You may be a native in your habitat,
But to foreigners you're just a foreigner.

THE PARENT

Children aren't happy with nothing to ignore,
And that's what parents were created for.

LINES TO BE MUTTERED THROUGH CLENCHED TEETH AND QUITE A LOT OF LATHER, IN THE COUNTRY

"Hark! Hark! The lark at Heaven's gate sings —"
Shut up, lark!
"And Phœbus 'gins arise —"
Sit down, Phœbus, before I knock you down!

Larks barking like beagles around a person's windows,
Sun-gods sneaking in at dawn and socking a person in
    the eye —
Why doesn't Nature go back to the Orient where it
    came from and bother the Mohammedans and
    Hindows
Instead of turning night into day every morning in
    Westchester County, N. Y.?

I speak for a community of commuters who toil for a
    pittance per diem —
Who spend 12 1/2 per cent of their waking lives on the
    N. Y., N. H., & H. —
Who would swap a billion shiny new A.M.'s for a
    secondhand P.M. —
I do not presume to speak for late risers such as Mr.
    Shubert and Mr. Winchell and Mr. Bache.
Why do we submit to a régime so tyrannical and
    despotic?
Why don't we do something about getting a lot less
    dawn and a lot more dusk?

I mean seriously, without any cracks about six months
of night in the Arctic —
Because I think if it could be arranged life would be
not nearly so grotusque.

Daybreak is one of the greatest disadvantages of living
under the solar system:
It means having to get up almost the very minute you
go to bed,
And bathe and shave and scrub industriously at your
molar system
And catch a train and go to the office and try to earn
some bread.

Come, let us leave the flowers and the birds and the
beasts to their sun-worship,
All of us human beings ought to be more skeptical than
a flower or a bird or a beast,
And a little serious thought should convince us that
sunshine is something to unworship
And that if we want to salute the daybreak we should
say not "Goodie goodie" but "Ah Cheest."

FAMILY COURT

One would be in less danger
From the wiles of the stranger
If one's own kin and kith
Were more fun to be with.

THE LIFE OF THE PARTY

Lily, there isn't a thing you lack,
Your effect is simply stunning.
But Lily, your gown is low in the back,
So conduct yourself with cunning.
Some of your charm is charm of face,
But some of your charm is spinal;
Losing your looks is no disgrace,
But losing your poise is final.
Ridicule's name is Legion,
So look to your dorsal region.

For Artie,
Old Artie,
The life of the party,
Is practically perfect tonight;
He's prettily, properly tight;
He's never appeared so bright.
Have you ever seen Artie
Enliven a party?
You've never seen Artie —
Why Lord love a duck!
At present old Artie is running amuck.
There's a wink in his eye
And a smile on his lips
For the matron he tickles,
The waiter he trips.
There's a rubber cigar,
And a smoking-room jest,

To melt the reserve
Of the clerical guest.
There's a pin for the man who stoops over,
And a little trained flea for Rover.
So Lily, beware of your back!
More daring than duller and older blades,
Artie is hot on the track.
I've noticed him eying your shoulderblades.
And maybe it's salad,
And maybe it's ice,
But I fear he has planned
Some amusing device,
For the laughter is slack
And he's taking it hard —
He's eying your back —
And Artie's a card —
He's forming a plan —
May I fetch you a shawl?
That inventive young man —
There is one in the hall.
Though your back is divine
In its natural state,
May I curtain your spine? —
Dear Heaven, I'm late!
Aren't you glad that you came to the party?
And weren't you amused by Artie?

Horace, the moment that you appeared,
I admired your manly beauty,
But I feel that a word about your beard

Is only my bounden duty.
Your tailor's craft is a dandy's dream,
Your suavity leaves me lyrical,
But escaping tonight with your self-esteem
Will require a minor miracle.
Fun is a gay deceiver,
So look to your kingly beaver.

For Artie,
Old Artie,
The life of the party,
Is hitting his stride tonight.
No bushel obscures his light.
He's knocking them left and right.
Have you ever seen Artie
Enliven a party?
You've never seen Artie —
My lad, you're in luck,
For Artie, old Artie, is running amuck.
At Artie's approach
Lesser wags droop.
Have you seen the tin roach
He drops in your soup?
Is a spoon in your pocket?
Or gum in your chair?
It's Artie, old Artie,
Who magicked them there.
And of those who complain, there's a rumor
That they're lacking in sense of humor.
So Horace, beware of your beard!

I scent some fantastic flubdubbery!
Old Artie has just disappeared
And I've noticed him eying your shrubbery.
And maybe it's syrup,
And maybe it's mice,
But I fear he has planned
Some amusing device.
His conceptions are weird,
And nothing is barred —
He was eying your beard —
And Artie's a card —
When Artie returns,
The fun will begin —
May I fetch you a bag
To put on your chin?
Just a small paper bag
To envelop the bait?
For Artie's a wag —
Dear Heaven, I'm late!
Aren't you glad that you came to the party?
And weren't you amused by Artie?

THE GERM

A mighty creature is the germ,
Though smaller than the pachyderm.
His customary dwelling place
Is deep within the human race.
His childish pride he often pleases
By giving people strange diseases.
Do you, my poppet, feel infirm?
You probably contain a germ.

ONE THIRD OF A CALENDAR

In January everything freezes.
We have two children. Both are she'ses.
This is our January rule:
One girl in bed, and one in school.

In February the blizzard whirls.
We own a pair of little girls.
Blessings upon of each the head —
The one in school and the one in bed.

March is the month of cringe and bluster.
Each of our children has a sister.
They cling together like Hansel and Gretel,
With their noses glued to the benzoin kettle.

April is made of impetuous waters
And doctors looking down throats of daughters.
If we had a son too, and a Samoyed,
We'd have a dog,
And a boy,
And two girls
In bed.

When people aren't asking questions
They're making suggestions
And when they're not doing one of those
They're either looking over your shoulder or stepping
    on your toes
And then as if that weren't enough to annoy you
They employ you.
Anybody at leisure
Incurs everybody's displeasure.
It seems to be very irking
To people at work to see other people not working,
So they tell you that work is wonderful medicine,
Just look at Firestone and Ford and Edison,
And they lecture you till they're out of breath or some-
    thing
And then if you don't succumb they starve you to
    death or something.
All of which results in a nasty quirk:
That if you don't want to work you have to work to
    earn enough money so that you won't have to
    work.

THE COW

The cow is of the bovine ilk;
One end is moo, the other, milk.

Mrs. Hattie Boomer Spink,
You puzzle me a lot.
Do you, I wonder, ever think?
And, if you do, of what?

Oh, solons bow like slender reeds
Beneath your firm resolve.
Your words I know, I know your deeds —
But whence do they evolve?

Do you employ a cerebrum,
And eke a cerebellum?
Or do you simply let 'em come,
With Gabriel at the hellum?

Nay, show me not your LL.D.
From Oklahoma Christian;
This honorary verdegree
Doth only beg the question.

Your native mental processes
Imply some secret canker;
Instead of thoughts, antipathies;
Instead of reason, rancor.

The ripple in your skull that spreads
From some primeval pebble,
How quickly washes o'er the heads
Of prophet and of rebel!

You three-name women, Mrs. Spink,
You puzzle me a lot.
Do you, I wonder, ever think?
And if you do, of what?

When gossip first began to link
Your name with that of Mr. Spink,
O Hattie Boomer, did you think?
— And what's become of Mr. Spink?

Oh, who would live in a silent house,
As still as a waltz left unwritten by Strauss,
As undisturbed as a virgin dewdrop,
And quiet enough to hear a shoe drop?
Who would dwell
In a vacuum cell,
In a home as mute as a clapperless bell?
Oh, a home as mute as a bell that's clapperless
Is forlorn as an Indian in Indianapolis.

Then ho! for the patter of little feet,
And the childish chatter of voices sweet,
For the ringing laughter and prancing capers
That soothe your ear as you read the papers,
For the trumpets that blow and the balls that bounce
As you struggle to balance your old accounts,
For the chubby arms that encircle your neck,
And the chubby behinds that your lap bedeck,
And sirens who save their wiliest wooing
For the critical spot in whatever you're doing.

Shakespeare's, I'm sure, was a silent house,
And that of Good King Wenceslaus,
And Napoleon's dwelling, and Alexander's,
And whoever's that wrote The Dog of Flanders.
Yes, Shelley and Keats
And other élites,
They missed the patter of little feets,

For he who sits and listens to pattering
Will never accomplish more than a smattering.

Then ho! for the patter of little feet!
Some find these footfalls doubly sweet,
Subjecting them to the twofold use
Of paternal pride and a good excuse.
You say, for instance, my modest chanteys
Are not so fine as Pope's or Dante's?
My deeds do not compare with those
Of Nelson, or Michelangelo's?
Well, my life is perpetual Children's Hour,
Or boy! would immortal genius flower!

GENEALOGICAL REFLECTION

No McTavish
Was ever lavish.

THE MIND OF PROFESSOR PRIMROSE

My story begins in the town of Cambridge, Mass.,
Home of the Harvard Business and Dental Schools,
And more or less the home of Harvard College.
Now, Harvard is a cultural institution,
Squandering many a dollar upon professors,
As a glance at a Harvard football team makes obvious;
Professors wise and prowling in search of wisdom,
And every mother's son of them absent-minded.
But the absentest mind belonged to Professor Primrose.
He had won a Nobel award and a Pulitzer Prize,
A Guggenheim and a leg on the Davis Cup,
But he couldn't remember to shave both sides of his
    face.
He discharged the dog and took the cook for an airing;
He frequently lit his hair and combed his cigar;
He set a trap for the baby and dandled the mice;
He wound up his key and opened the door with his
    watch;
He tipped his students and flunked the traffic police-
    man;
He fed the mosquitoes crumbs and slapped at the robins;
He always said his prayers when he entered the theater,
And left the church for a smoke between the acts;
He mixed the exterminator man a cocktail
And told his guests to go way, he had no bugs;
He rode the streets on a bicycle built for two,
And he never discovered he wasn't teaching at Yale.
At last one summer he kissed his crimson flannels

And packed his wife in camphor, and she complained.
She had always hated camphor, and she complained.
"My dear," she ordered, "these contretemps must cease;
You must bring this absent mind a little bit nearer;
You must tidy up that disorderly cerebellum;
You must write today and enroll in the Pelman Institute."
He embraced his pen and he took his wife in hand,
He wrinkled a stamp and thoughtfully licked his brow,
He wrote the letter and mailed it, and what do you know?
In a couple of days he disappeared from Cambridge.
"For heaven's sake, my husband has disappeared,"
Said Mrs. Primrose. "Now isn't that just like him?"
And she cut the meat and grocery orders in half,
And moved the chairs in the living room around,
And settled down to a little solid comfort.
She had a marvelous time for seven years,
At the end of which she took a train to Chicago.
She liked to go to Chicago once in a while
Because of a sister-in-law who lived in Cambridge.
Her eye was caught at Schenectady by the porter;
She noticed that he was brushing off a dime,
And trying to put the passenger in his pocket.
"Porter," she said, "aren't you Professor Primrose?
Aren't you my husband, the missing Professor Primrose?
And what did you learn at the Pelman Institute?"
"Mah Lawd, Maria," the porter said, "mah Lawd!
Did you say Pelman? Ah wrote to de Pullman folks!"

REFLECTION ON INGENUITY

Here's a good rule of thumb:
Too clever is dumb.

I ALWAYS SAY A GOOD SAINT IS NO
WORSE THAN A BAD COLD

Some sing of Alexander,
And some of Hercules,
And others sing of any old thing
They calculate will please.
O picayune, pallid bardlets,
Who peddle the spark divine!
Out of the way, while I fashion a lay
For good Saint Valentine.
For noble Valentine, tra-la!
For splendid Valentine!
I claim there ain't
Another Saint
As great as Valentine.

Some swear by Mother Pinkham,
And some by Father John,
While others shout for sauerkraut
To build their bodies on.
These patented Panaceas
Arouse no cheers of mine —
Let us rise in force and all endorse
The good Saint Valentine.
The genial Valentine, ta ra!
The kindly Valentine!
What can't be endured
Is quickly cured
By Doctor Valentine.

O you who woo the widow,
And you who woo the deb,
And you, and you, yes all who woo,
Give thanks for the middle of Feb.!
The coy and timorous creature
Who shrinks from your passionate line
Will leap from her cell like Ethel M. Dell
At a nod from Valentine.
From smiling Valentine, tra-la!
From virtuous Valentine!
We'd never annex
The female sex
Without Saint Valentine.

Elmer stops me in the street,
He fastens to my arm;
Elmer's words are words of heat,
I view him with alarm.
Elmer's eyes are eyes that glisten;
When he talks, he pants;
To Elmer's speech I do not listen;
Know it in advance.

Somewhere, somehow, something terrible,
Something altogether unbearable,
Squashes a premier, squashes a homebody,
Something dreadful happens to somebody.
Bombs are exploding like banks,
Banks are exploding like bombs,
Senators swallow their planks,
Kippurs are torn from their Yoms.
The world is adrift in a fog;
Myself, I am frankly appalled;
But Elmer is gayly agog;
Yes, Elmer is simply enthralled.
Says Elmer, the times are portentous,
We are favored to be on the spot
At a moment, he says, so momentous —
I trust he's momentously shot.

Elmer passes in the street,
I take him by the arm;

Elmer must have grown effete;
He views me with alarm.
Elmer's eyes are eyes that pop;
When I talk, he pants;
I orate without a stop;
Prepared it in advance.

Somewhere, somehow, something tedious,
Something stupidly yes-indeedious,
Something tiresome will happen to somebody,
Bore a celebrity, weary a homebody.
PM will yawn at The News,
The Dodgers lie down with the Giants,
Dictators will huddle in zoos,
And business will boom at Lane Bryant's.
Nothing will rise or fall
In a humdrum world and drowsy.
Elmer won't like it at all,
But life will be much less lousy.
I'm ragged from critical crises,
And I beg with my vanishing breath,
At the moment, O Lord, I want to be bored —
I want to be bored to death!

THE TURTLE

The turtle lives 'twixt plated decks
Which practically conceal its sex.
I think it clever of the turtle
In such a fix to be so fertile.

Come along, everybody, see the pretty baby,
Such a pretty baby ought to be adored.
Come along, everybody, come and bore the baby,
See the pretty baby, begging to be bored.

Hurry, hurry, Aunt Louise,
Silly names are sure to please.
Bother what the baby thinks!
Call her Kitchy-kitch and Binks,
Call her Wackywoo and Snookums,
Just ignore her dirty lookums,
Who than she is fairer game
For every kind of silly name?
Baby cannot answer back,
Or perhaps an aunt she'd lack.

Come along, everybody, isn't she a darling?
Such a little darling ought to be enjoyed.
Come along, everybody, let's annoy the baby,
Such a darling darling begs to be annoyed.

Goodness Gracious, Uncle George!
Home at last from Valley Forge?
Won't you try on her the whoops
That cheered the Continental troops?
Stand a little closer, please;
That will put her at her ease;
And babies find it hard to hear,

So place your mouth against her ear —
I guess she heard it, Uncle George;
I'm sure they did at Valley Forge.

Come along, everybody, see the little lady,
Isn't she adorable and kissable and pleasing?
Come along, everybody, come and tease the baby,
Here's a lady baby available for teasing!

Cousin Charles was always chummy;
He's about to poke her tummy.
Grandpa almost chokes on chuckles,
Tickling with his beard her knuckles;
All of Granny's muscles ache
From half an hour of patty-cake;
God-mamma with glee begins
A noisy count of baby's chins;
God-papa with humor glows
Playing piggie with her toes.
See the happy prideful parents,
Do they think of interference?
Certainly not, while baby gives
Such wholesome fun to relatives.

Up and at her, everybody, at the pretty baby,
Tell her she's a dumpling, tell her she's a dear.
Everybody knows the way to woo a baby —
Tickle her and pinch her and yodel in her ear.

What do you do when you've wedded a girl all legal
and lawful,
And she goes around saying she looks awful?
When she makes deprecatory remarks about her format,
And claims that her hair looks like a doormat?
When she swears that the complexion of which you
are so fond
Looks like the bottom of a dried-up pond?
When she for whom your affection is not the least like
Plato's
Compares her waist to a badly tied sack of potatoes?
When she thinks that every hour is the hour at which
avoirdupois begins,
And keeps discovering nonexistent double and triple
chins?
When she regrets her mouth,
And frowns at her nose for pointing North instead of
South?
Oh, who wouldn't rather be on a flimsy bridge with
a hungry lion at one end and a hungry tiger at the
other end and hungry crocodiles underneath
Than confronted by their dearest making remarks about
her own appearance through clenched teeth?
Oh, who wouldn't rather drown in the deepest ocean
or crackle in the most furious fire,
Than be in a position where if you say Yes darling, you
don't love her any more, and if you say No darling
you are a hypocritical liar?

Why won't they believe that the reason they find themselves the mother of your children is because you
think of all the looks in the world, their looks are
the nicest?
Why must we continue to be thus constantly ordealed
and crisised?
I think it high time these hoity-toity ladies were made
to realize that when they impugn their face and
their ankles and their waist
They are thereby insultingly impugning their tasteful
husbands' impeccable taste.

THE FISH

The fish, when he's exposed to air,
Displays no trace of savoir-faire,
But in the sea regains his balance
And exploits all his manly talents.
The chastest of the vertebrates,
He never even sees his mates,
But when they've finished, he appears
And O.K.'s all their bright ideas.

TELL IT TO THE ESKIMOS
or
TELL IT TO THE ESQUIMAUX

Jonathan Jukes is full of health,
And he doesn't care who knows it.
Others may exercise by stealth,
But he with a cry of Prosit!
Others put up with coated tongues,
And shoulders narrow and droopy;
Jonathan overinflates his lungs
With a thundering shout of Whoopee!
Jonathan's noise is healthy noise,
Jonathan's joys are healthy joys,
Jonathan shuns the primrose path,
And starts the day with an icy bath.

I might forgive the super-physique
Contained in the Jukes apparel;
The apple glowing in either cheek;
The chest like an oyster barrel;
The muscles that flow like a mountain stream,
The result of applied eugenics;
The rigorous diet, the stern régime
Of arduous calisthenics;
I can pardon most of the healthy joys,
I can pardon most of the healthy noise,
But Heaven itself no pardon hath
For the man who boasts of an icy bath.

If the Missing Links were vigorous chaps
And their manly deeds were myriad,
Must civilization then relapse
Back to the glacial period?
Humanity learns at a fearful price;
Must the lessons all be lost?
Does the locomotive feed on ice?
Is the liner propelled by frost?

One constant truth mankind has found
Through fire and flood and slaughter:
The thing that makes the wheels go round
Is plenty of good hot water.
And therefore, therefore, Jonathan Jukes,
You deserve the harshest of harsh rebukes;
You and your frigid daily bath
Are blocking civilization's path.
You think of yourself as Spartan and spunky?
So, Jonathan, is the old brass monkey.

Rain, rain, go away,
Come again another day,
Little Johnny wants to play.

Daddy's just as mad as hops
From looking at the dripping drops,
Daddy doesn't want the rain
To trickle on the windowpane.
Daddy wants an azure sky
And a fairway fast and dry;
He despises sodden turf
And water hazards full of surf.
When he sees a patch of blue
He practises his follow-through;
When the blue reverts to cloud,
Daddy's speech is rude and loud.
Sometimes with an angry shrug
He's putting putts along the rug;
Sometimes figuring out a plan
For murdering the weather man;
In either case it's more than plain
That Daddy doesn't like the rain.

Rain, rain, go away,
Come again another day,
Little Johnny wants to play.

Daddy may be cross, but ah!
Wait until you see Mamma!

She must do without her tennis
When the courts are bits of Venice.
I'm ashamed of what she mutters,
Gazing at the flooded gutters;
I'm afraid that she forgets
It's really raining violets;
That all these little silver drops
Bring the farmer bumper crops.
Mamma is angry when it pours;
She doesn't want to stay indoors.

Rain, rain, go away,
Come again another day,
Little Johnny wants to play.

Silly Johnny doesn't mind
By the weather being confined.
Drawing now, with might and main,
Pictures on the windowpane;
Choosing sides among the drops —
Some are robbers, some are cops.
Silly boy, for days together
He doesn't think about the weather.

REFLECTION ON CAUTION

Affection is a noble quality;
It leads to generosity and jollity.
But it also leads to breach of promise
If you go around lavishing it on red-hot momise.

I've never bet on a so-called horse
That the horse didn't lose a leg.
I've never putted on a golfing course
But the ball behaved like an egg.
I've never possessed three royal kings
But somebody held three aces;
In short, I'm a lad whose presence brings
The joy to bankers' faces.

And everybody says, "What a splendid loser!"
Everybody says, "What a thoroughgoing sport!"
And I smile my smile like an amiable Duse,
I leer like a lawyer in the presence of a tort.
And I crack my lips,
And I grin my grin,
While someone else
Rakes my money in.
Yes, I smile a smile like the Mona Lisa,
Though my spirits droop like the Tower of Pisa.
Yes, I chortle like a military march by Sousa
And everybody says, "What a splendid loser!"

I'll buy a tome, an expensive tome,
On the art of double dealing,
And I'll wrap it up and I'll take it home,
While the bells of Hell are pealing.
I'll stealthily study the ebony arts
Of men like the great Houdini,

Till both in foreign and local parts
I'm known as a darned old meany.

And everyone will say, "What a nasty winner!"
And everyone will say, "What a dreadful sport!"
And they'll all stop inviting me to come to dinner,
For I used to be a dimple and I want to be a wart.
But I won't care,
And I'll win with a scowl,
Foul means or fair,
But preferably foul.

I'll jeer my victims every time I vanquish,
And if I lose I shall scream with anguish.
And people will say, "What a dreadful sport!"
And I'll say, "Phooie!" or something of the sort.

People on whom I do not bother to dote
Are people who do not bother to vote.
Heaven forbid that they should ever be exempt
From contumely, obloquy and various kinds of contempt.
Some of them like Toscanini and some like Rudy Vallée,
But all of them take about as much interest in their right to ballot as their right to ballet.
They haven't voted since the heyday of Miss Russell (Lillian)
And excuse themselves by saying What's the difference of one vote in fifty million?
They have such refined and delicate palates
That they can discover no one worthy of their ballots,
And then when someone terrible gets elected
They say, There, that's just what I expected!
And they go around for four years spouting discontented criticisms
And contented witticisms,
And then when somebody to oppose the man they oppose gets nominated
They say Oh golly golly he's the kind of man I've always abominated,
And they have discovered that if you don't take time out to go to the polls
You can manage very nicely to get through thirty-six holes.

Oh let us cover these clever people very conspicuously
 with loathing,
For they are un-citizens in citizens' clothing.
They attempt to justify their negligence
On the grounds that no candidate appeals to people of
 their integligence,
But I am quite sure that if Abraham Lincoln (Rep.)
 ran against Thomas Jefferson (Dem.)
Neither man would be appealing enough to squeeze a
 vote out of them.

THE RHINOCEROS

The rhino is a homely beast,
For human eyes he's not a feast.
Farewell, farewell, you old rhinoceros,
I'll stare at something less prepoceros.

SEPTEMBER MORN

Oh, what in the world could be more fun
Than to have your holiday over and done;
Than to stand in a rural railway station
With fifty weeks till your next vacation!
Ah me, what jovial words are spoken
When you find the suitcase handle is broken.
You juggle golf bags and tennis rackets,
And ludicrous bulging paper packets,
You count your paraphernalia twice
From the children themselves to their milk and ice.
A whistle announces the train is coming;
You drop the children's portable plumbing;
The train draws up with a jerk and a wiggle
From the engineer's convulsive giggle,
And every window flattens the nose
Of a passenger reveling in your woes,
And the only car with an open door
Is a hundred yards behind or before.
Heave up the bags, the ice, the milk,
Heave up your struggling youthful ilk!
Heave up, heave up, and keep on heaving;
This good old train will soon be leaving.
The grim conductor, watch in hand,
Glares angrily on your hapless band.
Oh when was order e'er restored
By disgusted cries of All aboard?
This luggage on the platform piled
May well conceal a favorite child.

Conductor, cease your cry disgusted;
Distracted parents can't be trusted,
In times of stress they have been known
To ship their offspring off alone;
Not unprotected, not at large,
But in the kind conductor's charge.
Farewell, farewell to the sand and foam,
You are getting yourself and your family home.
Oh, I think there is no such capital fun
But having your teeth out one by one.

I know that a little verse is a versicle but I don't know
    if a little phrase is a phrasicle

But I do know that at the moment I feel too too alas
    and alackadaisicle.

What though around me is the hustle and bustle of a
    great city at its labors?

What though I am hemmed in by the most industrious
    and ingenious kind of neighbors?

What though young people are joining forever or part-
    ing forever with each tick of the clock?

What though Mr. Belloc admires Mr. Chesterton or
    Mr. Chesterton admires Mr. Belloc?

What though to produce the Sunday papers thousands
    of square miles of Canada are deforested?

What though in an attempt to amuse the public thou-
    sands of writers and actors and things are utterly
    exhorested?

What though young humans are getting born and old
    humans are getting deceased and middle-aged hu-
    mans are getting used to it?

What though a Bronxville husband has discovered that
    he can put the baby to sleep by reading Proust to it?

All these things may be of great moment to those who
    are concerned with them in any way,

But how are they going to help me to get through the
    day?

For I have had to eat luncheon while I was still sorry

I had eaten breakfast and I shall have to eat dinner
    while I am still sorry I ate luncheon
And my spirit has been put through the third degree
    and thrown into a very dark dank dismal duncheon.
Why do people insist on bringing me anecdotes and
    allegories and alcohol and food?
Why won't they just let me sit and brood?
Why does the population swirl around me with vivacious
    violence
When all I want to do is sit and suffer in siolence?
Everybody I see tries to cheer me up
And I wish they would stop.

REFLECTION ON BABIES

A bit of talcum
Is always walcum.

Some of us remember
Carriages and horses,
Some of us remember
The days before divorces.
Some of us remember
"Mr. Dooley says,"
But none of us can recollect
A G. O. Party Pres.

Republicans are handsome, Republicans are good,
But Democrats are President, that is understood.
Republicans, Republicans are ragged and forlorn.
Democrats, Democrats are to the manna born.

Turnabout and turnabout
Is good fair play.
Cats may look at royalty,
Dogs deserve a day,
The lowly shall inherit,
But everybody says
Bouncing wee Republicans
Never will be Pres.

Republicans are kindly, Republicans are bright,
But Democrats are President, that is only right.
Republicans, Republicans are ragged and forlorn.
Democrats, Democrats are to the manna born.

When I was but a boy,
'Twas my once-a-yearly joy
To arise of a Yuletide morning,
And eagerly behold
The crimson and the gold
Of the messages the mantelpiece adorning.
There were angels, there were squires,
There were steeples, there were spires,
There were villagers, and mistletoe and holly,
There were cosy English inns
With the snow around their chins,
And I innocently thought them rather jolly.
I blush for me, but by your leave,
I'm afraid that I am still naïve.

Oh, give me an old-fashioned Christmas card,
With mistletoe galore, and holly by the yard,
With galumptious greens and gorgeous scarlets,
With crackling logs and apple-cheeked varlets,
With horses prancing down a frosty road,
And a stagecoach laden with a festive load,
And the light from the wayside windows streaming,
And a white moon rising and one star gleaming.

Departed is the time
Of Christmases sublime;
My soprano is now a mezzo-basso;
And the mantelpiece contains

The angular remains
Of a later representative Picasso.
There are circles, there are dots,
There are corners, there are spots,
There are modernistic snapshots of the city;
Or, when the artist lags,
They are livened up with gags.
You must choose between the arty and the witty.
I blush for me, but I must say
I wish you'd take them all away.

Oh, give me an old-fashioned Christmas card,
With hostlers hostling in an old inn yard,
With church bells chiming their silver notes,
And jolly red squires in their jolly red coats,
And a good fat goose by the fire that dangles,
And a few more angels and a few less angles.
Turn backward, Time, to please this bard,
And give me an old-fashioned Christmas card.

BIRTH COMES TO THE ARCHBISHOP

Ministers
Don't like bar sinisters.
They consider that sort of irregularity
As the height of vulgarity
And go around making remarks
About the need for patrolling the beaches and parks.
They hate to see any deadlock
Between sin and wedlock
And get very nervous
When people omit the marriage service.
They regard as villains
Owners of unauthorized chillains,
A point of view
Which of course doesn't embarrass me or you
But makes things very inconvenient
For many really quite nice girls who may have been just
    a bit lenient.

So although none of us is in danger
Of the arrival of an inexplicable little stranger
Still I think we ought to join with a lot of others
And wish the best of luck to the nation's unmarried
    mothers.

Ichneumons are fond of little ichneumons,
And lions of little lions,
But I am not fond of little humans;
I do not believe in scions.

Of course there's always our child,
But our child is different,
Our child appeals
To the cultivated mind.
Ours is a lady;
Boys are odoriferant;
Ladies are the sweetness;
Boys are the rind.

Whenever whimsy collides with whimsy
As parents compare their cherubs,
At the slightest excuse, however flimsy,
I fold my tent like the Arubs.

Of course there's always our child,
But our child is charminger,
Our child's eyes
Are a special kind of blue;
Our child's smile
Is quite a lot disarminger;
Our child's tooth
Is very nearly through.

Mankind, I consider, attained its zenith
The day it achieved the adult;

When the conversation to infants leaneth,
My horse is bridled and saddult.

Of course there's always our child,
But our child is wittier;
Our child's noises
Are the nicest kind of noise;
She has no beard
Like Tennyson or Whittier;
But Tennyson and Whittier
Began as little boys.

The Politician, the Parent, the Preacher,
Were each of them once a kiddie.
The child is indeed a talented creature.
Do I want one? Oh God forbidde!

Of course there's always our child
But our child's adorable.
Our child's an angel
Fairer than the flowers;
Our child fascinates
One who's rather borable;
And incidentally,
Our child is ours.

OLD MEN

People expect old men to die,
They do not really mourn old men.
Old men are different. People look
At them with eyes that wonder when . . .
People watch with unshocked eyes;
But the old men know when an old man dies.

A DRINK WITH SOMETHING IN IT

There is something about a Martini,
A tingle remarkably pleasant;
A yellow, a mellow Martini;
I wish that I had one at present.
There is something about a Martini,
Ere the dining and dancing begin,
And to tell you the truth,
It is not the vermouth —
I think that perhaps it's the gin.

There is something about an old-fashioned
That kindles a cardiac glow;
It is soothing and soft and impassioned
As a lyric by Swinburne or Poe.
There is something about an old-fashioned
When dusk has enveloped the sky,
And it may be the ice,
Or the pineapple slice,
But I strongly suspect it's the rye

There is something about a mint julep.
It is nectar imbibed in a dream,
As fresh as the bud of the tulip,
As cool as the bed of the stream.
There is something about a mint julep,
A fragrance beloved by the lucky.
And perhaps it's the tint
Of the frost and the mint,
But I think it was born in Kentucky.

There is something they put in a highball
That awakens the torpidest brain,
That kindles a spark in the eyeball,
Gliding singing through vein after vein.
There is something they put in a highball
Which you'll notice one day, if you watch;
And it may be the soda,
But judged by the odor,
I rather believe it's the Scotch.

Then here's to the heartening wassail,
Wherever good fellows are found;
Be its master instead of its vassal,
And order the glasses around.
For there's something they put in the wassail
That prevents it from tasting like wicker;
Since it's not tapioca,
Or mustard, or mocha,
I'm forced to conclude it's the liquor.

WATCHMAN, WHAT OF THE FIRST
FIRST LADY?

Everybody can tell you the date of George Washing-
    ton's birth,
But who knows the date on which Mrs. George Wash-
    ington first appeared on earth?
Isn't there any justice
For the former Mrs. Custis?
Of course her memory is perpetuated by a hotel,
But Hell.
It's a disgrace to every United State
That we don't know more about our first president's
    only mate.
We all know a lot of stories about the wife of King
    Arthur
But you never hear any about Martha.
And we have all read a lot of romantic tales about
    Catherine the Great,
But nobody even writes them about Washington's mate.
And we have all seen Katharine Cornell, or was it
    Helen Hayes or Ethel Barrymore,
Impersonate Cleopatra, who wasn't even anybody's real
    wife but nothing more or less than a promiscuous
    un-American parrymore,
But has anybody done anything about the mistress of
    the nation's whitest house?
No, and yet but for her the nation would be the child
    of a man without a spouse.

May I join you in the doghouse, Rover?
I wish to retire till the party's over.
Since three o'clock I've done my best
To entertain each tiny guest;
My conscience now I've left behind me,
And if they want me, let them find me.
I blew their bubbles, I sailed their boats,
I kept them from each other's throats.
I told them tales of magic lands,
I took them out to wash their hands.
I sorted their rubbers and tied their laces,
I wiped their noses and dried their faces.
Of similarity there's lots
'Twixt tiny tots and Hottentots.
I've earned repose to heal the ravages
Of these angelic-looking savages.
Oh, progeny playing by itself
Is a lonely fascinating elf,
But progeny in roistering batches
Would drive St. Francis from here to Natchez.
Shunned are the games a parent proposes;
They prefer to squirt each other with hoses,
Their playmates are their natural foemen
And they like to poke each other's abdomen.
Their joy needs another's woe to cushion it
Say a puddle, and somebody littler to push in it.
They observe with glee the ballistic results
Of ice cream with spoons for catapults,

And inform the assembly with tears and glares
That everyone's presents are better than theirs.
Oh, little women and little men,
Someday I hope to love you again,
But not till after the party's over,
So give me the key to the doghouse, Rover.

THE PANTHER

The panther is like a leopard,
Except it hasn't been peppered.
Should you behold a panther crouch,
Prepare to say Ouch.
Better yet, if called by a panther,
Don't anther.

I observe, as I hold my lonely course,
That nothing exists without a source.
Thus, oaks from acorns, lions from cubs,
And health and wealth from the proper clubs.
There are yacht clubs, golf clubs, clubs for luncheon,
Clubs for flowing bowl and puncheon,
Clubs for dancing, clubs for gambling,
Clubs for sociable Sunday ambling,
Clubs for imbibing literature,
And clubs for keeping the cinema pure,
Clubs for friendship, clubs for snobbery,
Clubs for smooth political jobbery.
As civilization onward reels,
It's clubs that grease the speeding wheels.

Alas!

Oh, everybody belongs to something,
But I don't belong to anything;
No, I don't belong to anything, any more than the
        miller of Dee,
And everything seems to belong
To people who belong to something,
But I don't belong to anything,
So nothing belongs to me.

Racquet, Knickerbocker, Union League,
Shriners parading without fatigue,

Oddfellows, Red Men, Woodmen of the World,
Solvent Moose and Elks dew-pearled,
Tammany tigers, Temperance doves,
Groups of various hates and loves,
Success is the thing they all have an air of,
Theirs are the tickets that are taken care of,
Theirs are the incomes but not the taxes,
Theirs are the sharpest, best-ground axes;
Millions of members of millions of bands,
Greeting fellow members with helping hands;
Good fellows all in incorporated hordes,
Prosperity is what they are moving towards.

Alas!

Oh, everybody belongs to something,
But I don't belong to anything;
Yes, I belong to nothing at all, from Kiwanis to the
     R.F.C.,
And everything definitely belongs
To people who belong to lots of things,
But I don't belong to anything,
So nothing belongs to me.

PEDIATRIC REFLECTION

Many an infant that screams like a calliope
Could be soothed by a little attention to its diope.

MACBETH HAS MURDERED SLEEP?

or

DON'T MAKE ME LAUGH

The ravelled sleeve of care, O Sleep,
Knit up or not. I shall not weep.
Make up your mind, or leave it lay,
I'm fortified, whichever way.
Farewell, farewell to Morpheus' arms!
Welcome excursions and alarms!
Murder will out, so will the night,
Far sooner than this bedside light.
When borogoves grow over-mimsy,
Destroy them with Lord Peter Wimsey;
When landlords lurk upon the morrow,
Sneer Gallicly with Hercule Poirot,
Or with your thumb in some forlorn dyke,
Refresh your soul with Doctor Thorndyke.
Let Strephon dream of merry maying,
I much prefer a ghastly slaying.
I find myself a sounder man
For Father Brown and Charlie Chan.
I hug myself and holler "Champion!"
When I encounter Albert Campion;
To me like the Golden Fleece to Jason
Are Inspector French and Perry Mason,
And blissful am I when a handler
Of anything by Raymond Chandler.
Indeed I'll even take a chance
On Ellery Queen and Philo Vance,

Enduring barely in the latter
The mannerisms for the matter.
More soothing than the genial toddy
I hold a mutilated body.
I've watched with fascinated eyes
Detectives fall, detectives rise,
And racing through a thousand tomes,
Reflect, There's no police like Holmes.

GOOD–BY, OLD YEAR, YOU OAF

or

WHY DON'T THEY PAY THE BONUS?

Many of the three hundred and sixty-five days of the
    year are followed by dreadful nights but one night
    is by far, oh yes, by far the worst,

And that, my friends, is the night of December the
    thirty-first.

Man can never get it through his head that he is born
    to be not a creditor but a debtor;

Man always thinks the annual thought that just be-
    cause last year was terrible next year is bound to
    be better.

Man is a victim of dope

In the incurable form of hope;

Man is a blemishless Pollyanna,

And is convinced that the advent of every New Year
    will place him in possession of a bumper crop of
    manna.

Therefore Man fills himself up with a lot of joie de vivre

And goes out to celebrate New Year's Ivre;

Therefore millions of respectable citizens who just a
    week before have been perfectly happy to sit at
    home and be cosily Christmas carolized

Consider it a point of honor to go out on the town
    and get themselves paralyzed;

Therefore the whistles blow toot toot and the bells ring
    ding ding and the confetti goes confetti confetti at
    midnight on the thirty-first of December,

And on January first the world is full of people who
either can't and wish they could, or can and wish
they couldn't remember.

They never seem to learn from experience;

They keep on doing it year after year from the time
they are puling infants till they are doddering oc-
togenerience.

My goodness, if there's anything in heredity and en-
vironment

How can people expect the newborn year to manifest
any culture or refironment?

Every New Year is the direct descendant, isn't it, of a
long line of proven criminals?

And you can't turn it into a philanthropist by welcom-
ing it with cocktails and champagne any more suc-
cessfully than with prayer books and hyminals.

Every new year is a country as barren as the old one, and
it's no use trying to forage it;

Every new year is incorrigible; then all I can say is
for Heaven's sakes, why go out of your way to
incorrage it?

A CAROL FOR CHILDREN

God rest you, merry Innocents,
Let nothing you dismay,
Let nothing wound an eager heart
Upon this Christmas day.

Yours be the genial holly wreaths,
The stockings and the tree;
An aged world to you bequeaths
Its own forgotten glee.

Soon, soon enough come crueler gifts,
The anger and the tears;
Between you now there sparsely drifts
A handful yet of years.

Oh, dimly, dimly glows the star
Through the electric throng;
The bidding in temple and bazaar
Drowns out the silver song.

The ancient altars smoke afresh,
The ancient idols stir;
Faint in the reek of burning flesh
Sink frankincense and myrrh.

Gaspar, Balthazar, Melchior!
Where are your offerings now?
What greetings to the Prince of War,
His darkly branded brow?

Two ultimate laws alone we know,
The ledger and the sword —
So far away, so long ago,
We lost the infant Lord.

Only the children clasp his hand;
His voice speaks low to them,
And still for them the shining band
Wings over Bethlehem.

God rest you, merry Innocents,
While innocence endures.
A sweeter Christmas than we to ours
May you bequeath to yours.

SONG FOR A TEMPERATURE OF A
HUNDRED AND ONE

Of all God's creatures give me man
For impractical uniqueness,
He's hardly tenth when it comes to strength,
But he leads the field in weakness.
Distemper suits the ailing dog,
The chicken's content with pip,
But the human race, which sets the pace,
Takes nothing less than Grippe.

THEN, hey for the grippe, for the goodly la grippe!
In dogs it's distemper, in chickens it's pip;
But the lords of creation insist at the least
On the germ that distinguishes man from the beast.

The mule with mange is satisfied,
Or hookworm in the South;
And the best-bred kine will stand in line
To get their hoof-and-mouth;
Bubonic cheers the humble rat
As he happily leaves the ship;
When the horse gets botts he thinks it's lots,
But people hold out for grippe.
THEN, hey for the grippe, for the goodly la grippe,
For the frog in the throat and the chap on the lip;
For the ice on the feet and the fire on the brow,
And the bronchial tubes that moo like a cow.
And hey for the ache in the back of the legs,

And the diet of consommé, water and eggs,
For the mustard that sits on your chest like a cactus,
For the doctor you're kindly providing with practus;
And hey for the pants of which you're so fond,
And the first happy day they're allowed to be donned;
For the first day at work, all bundled in wraps,
And last but not least, for the splendid relapse.
So let man meet his Maker, a smile on his lip,
Singing hey, double hey, for the goodly la grippe.

WHAT'S THE USE?

Sure, deck your lower limbs in pants;
Yours are the limbs, my sweeting.
You look divine as you advance —
Have you seen yourself retreating?

I know lots of men who are in love and lots of men who
    are married and lots of men who are both,
And to fall out with their loved ones is what all of
    them are most loth.
They are conciliatory at every opportunity,
Because all they want is serenity and a certain amount
    of impunity.
Yes, many the swain who has finally admitted that the
    earth is flat
Simply to sidestep a spat,
Many the masculine Positively or Absolutely which has
    been diluted to an If
Simply to avert a tiff,
Many the two-fisted executive whose domestic con-
    versation is limited to a tactfully interpolated Yes,
And then he is amazed to find that he is being raked
    backwards over a bed of coals nevertheless.
These misguided fellows are under the impression that
    it takes two to make a quarrel, that you can side-
    step a crisis by nonaggression and nonresistance,
Instead of removing yourself to a discreet distance.
Passivity can be a provoking modus operandi;
Consider the Empire and Gandhi.
Silence is golden, but sometimes invisibility is golder,
Because loved ones may not be able to make bricks
    without straw but often they don't need any straw
    to manufacture a bone to pick or blood in their eye
    or a chip for their soft white shoulder.

It is my duty, gentlemen, to inform you that women are dictators all, and I recommend to you this moral: In real life it takes only one to make a quarrel.

ONE, TWO, BUCKLE MY SHOE

Roses red and jonquils gold,
I know a girl who is two years old.
Hyacinth white and violets blue,
She was very good, so now she's two.
The rabbit there on the corner shelf,
He wishes that he were two, himself,
And Little Bo Peep on the silver cup
Says, "Gracious, Linell is growing up!"
And the faithful music box simply burns
To wish her many happy returns.
The cows in the meadow murmur, "Moo!
To think that child has arrived at two!"
The cows in the meadow moo and mutter,
And send their specialest milk and butter.
The cardinal on the window sill
Greets the news with an extra trill,
The mockingbird and the dandy jay
With kindest respects salute the day,
And the swaggering crow admits his awe,
Cawing a splendid birthday caw,
And the squirrel hoists his bushy tail
In the squirrel manner of crying "Hail!"

Roses red and violets blue,
I know a girl who is really two.
Yesterday she was only one;
Today, I think, will be twice the fun.
For all good things come double fold

When a good girl gets to be two years old.
Double the number of stairs to climb,
And maybe some of them two at a time;
Double the songs and double the dances,
Double the grave and merry fancies;
Double the dolls to undress and scrub,
Double the ducks in the evening tub;
Double walks in exciting lanes,
And double trips to wave at the trains;
And certainly, double stories told
When a good girl gets to be two years old.
Linell, Linell, is it really true?
Do you faithfully promise that you are two?
Kiss me again for a lucky start
And Happy Birthday, with twice my heart!

THE KITTEN

The trouble with a kitten is
THAT
Eventually it becomes a
CAT.

LET GEORGE DO IT, IF YOU CAN
FIND HIM

The wind comes walloping out of the West,
And the sky is lapis lazuli,
And the hills are bold in red and gold,
And I cannot take it casually.
Oh, cruel day for a man to spend
At counter or desk or forge!
I think I shall stray from duty today,
And turn it over to George.

George! George! Where are you, George?
Clear the air for a call to George!
There is work to be done, dear George,
And fame to be won, dear George!
There are words to write,
And columns to add,
And everyone says
That George is the lad.
Here is a pen and here is a pencil,
Here's a typewriter, here's a stencil,
Here is a list of today's appointments,
And all the flies in all the ointments,
The daily woes that a man endures —
Take them, George, they're yours!

I will arise and roam the fields
Where edible coveys flutter,
I will conquer, methinks, the perilous links

With a true and deadly putter.
I'll forsake the grime of the city street
For valley and hill and gorge;
I will, or would, or I shall, or should,
But I can't get hold of George!

George! George! Where are you, George?
Come out from under the sofa, George!
I thought you were braver, George!
I'm doing you a favor, George!
You can use my desk,
And sit in my chair,
Snugly away
From the nasty air.
Safe from the other fellow's cartridges,
Safe from returning without any partridges,
Safe from treacherous spoons and brassies,
And the flaming shorts of the golfing lassies.
All this, dear George, I am trying to spare you.
George! You softie, where are you?

Personally I don't care whether a detective-story writer
 was educated in night school or day school
So long as they don't belong to the H.I.B.K. school.
The H.I.B.K. being a device to which too many detective-story writers are prone,
Namely the Had I But Known.
Sometimes it is the Had I But Known what grim secret
 lurked behind that smiling exterior I would never
 have set foot within the door,
Sometimes the Had I But Known then what I know
 now I could have saved at least three lives by
 revealing to the Inspector the conversation I heard
 through that fortuitous hole in the floor.
Had-I-But-Known narrators are the ones who hear a
 stealthy creak at midnight in the tower where the
 body lies, and, instead of locking their door or
 arousing the drowsy policeman posted outside their
 room, sneak off by themselves to the tower and
 suddenly they hear a breath exhaled behind them,
And they have no time to scream, they know nothing
 else till the men from the D.A.'s office come in
 next morning and find them.
Had I But Known-ers are quick to assume the preroga-
 tives of the Deity,
For they will suppress evidence that doesn't suit their
 theories with appalling spontaneity,
And when the killer is finally trapped into a confession
 by some elaborate device of the Had I But

Known-er some hundred pages later than if they
hadn't held their knowledge aloof,
Why they say Why Inspector I knew all along it was
he but I couldn't tell you, you would have laughed
at me unless I had absolute proof.
Would you like a nice detective story for your library
which I am sorry to say I didn't rent but owns?
I wouldn't have bought it had I but known it was im-
pregnated with Had I But Knowns.

THE CARIBOU

Among the forests of the North,
The caribou walks back and forth.
The North is full of antlered game,
But none so pervious to fame.
For sportsmen on a sporting quest,
The caribou leads all the rest.
I hardly dare to tell you, madam,
I call him Caribou Ben Adhem.

LET'S NOT GO TO THE THEATER TONIGHT
or
WE COULDN'T GET SEATS ANYHOW

Light the lights at four o'clock, pull the curtains down,
Turn the radiator on, winter walks the town.
The speculators waken, and the critics are unloosed,
And all the summer theaters are coming home to roost.
For the drama has departed from Ogunquit,
The audience has vanished from Wiscasset,
And instead of city strangers
There is hay among the mangers
Of Skowhegan, and Carmel, and Cohasset.
Oh, when is a barn not a barn?
Riddle me this, I pray.
Why, not from about the middle of June
Till after Labor Day.
The evicted cows in the rain must browse
Till after Labor Day.

Order dinner early, dear, and robe yourself in style
As I telephone the broker for a couple on the aisle.
But hear the broker chuckle as he warbles like a finch,
There's nothing left but standing room, at eleven dol-
    lars an inch.
For the natives swarm upon us from Nantucket,
They throng from Painted Post and Triple Fork,
They've abandoned Martha's Vineyard
For Manhattan's fertile sin yard,
They are going to the theater in New York.

Oh, when is a theater not a theater?
This is my wistful tune.
Why, not from after October first
Till around the middle of June.
You can't sit down at a play in town
Till around the middle of June.

So pack your evening gown away, unwave your wavèd
    hair,
No need to brave the traffic of Mr. Times's Square.
The show we cannot see tonight for money or for love
Will adorn our local silo after June the middle of.
Then it's Ho! for Shaw and Shakespeare in Ogunquit,
And Connelly and Kaufman in Wiscasset!
We will take our Sidney Howard,
Our Maugham and Noel Coward,
In comfort, and Skowhegan, and Cohasset.
Oh, when is a play not a play?
And if it be thus, how be it?
Well, it's my belief that it's not a play
If you can't get in to see it.
So suppose we wait for a summer date,
And sit in a barn to see it.

Mother's Day is a very fine day,
And mothers are very fine people,
And the human race by them is crowned
As the church is crowned by the steeple.
We often refer to mother love;
To mother hate, less often;
To fathers we hardly refer at all,
But once a year we soften.

It's Father's Day, it's Father's Day,
The eager mothers cry.
And what of that? And what of that?
The fathers make reply.
Well, here's a collar, and here's a stud,
The mothers murmur low,
And fathers avoid each other's glance,
Meaning, I told you so.

Oh, Mother's Day is a very fine day,
And not alone for mothers.
The florist finds it to his taste,
And so do a lot of others.
The candy people jump for joy,
The jeweller rubs his hands,
And the new coupé is shining proof
That Father understands.

It's Mother's Day, it's Mother's Day,
The eager fathers cry,

And, Red-hot diggety ziggety dog,
The mothers make reply.
Well, here's a wrap of sable fur,
The fathers murmur low,
And mothers catch each other's glance,
Meaning, I told you so.

Oh, Father's Day is a dreadful day,
And therefore fathers dread it;
For better a cycle of calm neglect
Than a day of grudging credit.
Oh why not leave the fathers be?
Their point of view is stoic;
So let them lurk in their niche in life,
Essential but not heroic.

LEGAL REFLECTION

The postal authorities of the United States of America
Frown on Curiosa, Erotica and Esoterica,
Which is a break, I guess,
For stockholders of the American Railway Express.

There is at least one thing I would less rather have in
the neighborhood than a gangster,
And that one thing is a practical prankster.
I feel that we should differ more sharply than Mon-
tagues and Capulets or York and Lancaster,
Me and a practical prancaster.
If there is a concentration camp in limbo, that is the
spot for which I nominate them,
Not because I don't like them, but simply because I
abominate them.
The born practical prankster starts out in early youth
by offering people a chair,
And when they sit down it isn't there,
And he is delighted and proceeds to more complicated
wheezes,
Such as ten cent X-rays to see through people's clothes
with and powders to give them itches and sneezes,
And his boutonnière is something that people get
squirted in the eye out of,
And their beds are what he makes apple pie out of.
Then as he matures he widens his scope,
And he is no longer content to present people with
exploding cigars and chocolate creams with centers
of soap,
So he dresses up as an Oriental potentate and reviews
the British fleet.

I have recently read with complete satisfaction of a
    practical prankster two of whose friends had just
    been married,
Which was of course in itself simply a challenge to be
    harried,
And it was a challenge he was eager to meet,
And he went to the roof of their hotel and tied a rope
    around his waist and a colleague lowered him to
    where he could clash a pair of cymbals outside
    the window of the nuptial suite,
And he weighed two hundred and eighty pounds and
    the rope broke,
And that to my mind is the perfect practical joke.

LUCY LAKE

Lawsamassy, for heaven's sake!
Have you never heard of Lucy Lake?
Lucy is fluffy and fair and cosy,
Lucy is like a budding posy.
Lucy speaks with a tiny lisp,
Lucy's mind is a will-o'-the-wisp.
Lucy is just as meek as a mouse,
Lucy lives in a darling house,
With a darling garden and darling fence,
And a darling faith in the future tense.
A load of hay, or a crescent moon,
And she knows that things will be better soon.
Lucy resigns herself to sorrow
In building character for tomorrow.
Lucy tells us to carry on,
It's always darkest before the dawn.
A visit to Lucy's bucks you up,
Helps you swallow the bitterest cup.
Lucy Lake is meek as a mouse.
Let's go over to Lucy's house,
And let's lynch Lucy!

THE OYSTER

The oyster's a confusing suitor;
It's masc., and fem., and even neuter.
But whether husband, pal or wife
It leads a painless sort of life.
I'd like to be an oyster, say,
In August, June, July or May.

HOW LONG HAS THIS BEEN GOING ON?
OH, QUITE LONG

Some people think that they can beat three two's with
    a pair of aces,

And other people think they can wind up ahead of
    the races,

And lest we forget,

The people who think they can wind up ahead of the
    races are everybody who has ever won a bet.

Yes, when you first get back five-sixty for two, oh what
    a rosy-toed future before you looms,

But actually your doom is sealed by whoever it is that
    goes around sealing people's dooms,

And you are lost forever

Because you think you won not because you were lucky
    but because you were clever.

You think the race ended as it did, not because you
    hoped it,

But because you doped it,

And from then on you withdraw your savings from the
    bank in ever-waxing wads

Because you are convinced that having figured out one
    winner you can figure out many other winners at
    even more impressive odds,

And pretty soon overdrawing your account or not bet-
    ting at all is the dilemma which you are betwixt

And certainly you're not going to not bet at all be-
    cause you are sure you will eventually wind up
    ahead because the only reason the races haven't

run true to form, by which you mean your form,
    is because they have been fixed,
So all you need to be a heavy gainer
Is to bet on one honest race or make friends with one
    dishonest trainer.
And I don't know for which this situation is worse,
Your character or your purse.
I don't say that race tracks are centers of sin,
I only say that they are only safe to go to as long as
    you fail to begin to win.

The weather is so very mild
That some would call it warm.
Good gracious, aren't we lucky, child?
Here comes a thunderstorm.

The sky is now indelible ink,
The branches reft asunder;
But you and I, we do not shrink;
We love the lovely thunder.

The garden is a raging sea,
The hurricane is snarling;
Oh happy you and happy me!
Isn't the lightning darling?

Fear not the thunder, little one.
It's weather, simply weather;
It's friendly giants full of fun
Clapping their hands together.

I hope of lightning our supply
Will never be exhausted;
You know it's lanterns in the sky
For angels who are losted.

We love the kindly wind and hail,
The jolly thunderbolt,
We watch in glee the fairy trail
Of ampere, watt, and volt.

Oh, than to enjoy a storm like this
There's nothing I would rather.
Don't dive beneath the blankets, Miss!
Or else leave room for Father.

THE WAPITI

There goes the Wapiti,
Hippety-hoppity!

HEARTS AND FLOWERS

or

WHAT I KNOW ABOUT BOLIVAR BLACK

I do not care for Bolivar Black,
And I think that I never shall;
A shiver goes rippling up my back
When Bolivar calls me Pal.
I am commonly captain of my soul,
But my head is bowed and bloody,
No joy can I find in human kind,
When Bolivar calls me Buddy.

His smile is broad as the Golden West
From Olympia, Wash., to Texas,
And a heart as warm as a desert storm
Sizzles his solar plexus.
Bolivar's love for his fellow man
Is deep as the rolling ocean,
And the favorite scent of the Orient
Enlivens his shaving lotion.

He's wild about kiddies, people say,
And devoted to widows and orphans;
When he speaks as he should of motherhood
His sonorous accent sorftens.
He scatters crumbs for our feathered friends,
He is kind to kittens and puppies,
And his salary check is at the beck
Of a prodigal tribe of guppies.

The beggars gamble among themselves
For the right to beg of Bolivar;
And the yeggmen go with a tale of woe
Instead of a big revolivar.
He lavishes fruit on his travelling friends,
And flowers upon the ill;
When a dozen dine and order wine,
Why, Bolivar grabs the bill.

His virtues bloom like the buds in May,
His faults, I believe, are few,
But whether you find him gold or clay
Depends on the point of view.
So you may care for Bolivar Black,
And his generous actions quote;
My praise is checked when I recollect
My name on Bolivar's note.

I sit in an office at 244 Madison Avenue,

And say to myself You have a responsible job, havenue?

Why then do you fritter away your time on this dog-
gerel?

If you have a sore throat you can cure it by using a
good goggeral,

If you have a sore foot you can get it fixed by a chiro-
podist,

And you can get your original sin removed by St. John
the Bopodist,

Why then should this flocculent lassitude be incurable?

Kansas City, Kansas, proves that even Kansas City
needn't always be Missourible.

Up up my soul! This inaction is abominable.

Perhaps it is the result of disturbances abdominable.

The pilgrims settled Massachusetts in 1620 when they
landed on a stone hummock.

Maybe if they were here now they would settle my
stomach.

Oh, if I only had the wings of a bird

Instead of being confined on Madison Avenue I could
soar in a jiffy to Second or Third.

Ha ha ha! the sun is shining!
Yo ho ho! the sky is blue!
See the earth in peace reclining!
See the ocean reclining, too!
Tra la la! the birds are chirruping!
Fields are green and flowers are gay!
Maples swell with sap a-syruping!
Nature is spreading herself today!

Well, let's go out and trample on a violet,
Let's steal candy from a curly-headed tot,
Take a wrong number and deliberately dial it,
Let's plant thistles under squatters when they squat,
Let's throw pepper on the robins on their nests,
Let's tell Altman's we prefer to buy at Best's,
Let's cry Boo! at golfers as they putt,
Let's open windows that people want shut,
Let's step on somebody's nice white shoes,
Let's join a club and not pay dues,
Let's send bills and let's raise rents,
Let's put mosquitoes in campers' tents,
Let's teach Nature not to spread so free
On a day when my love is off of me.

Yah yah yah! the rain is raining!
Zut alors! the wild waves boil!
Hear the homeless wind complaining!
Watch the shrubbery bite the soil!

Nya nya nya! come sleet, come icicles!
The world is a welter of freezing spray!
Pity the sailors on their high-wheeled bicycles!
Nature is having a tantrum today!

Well, let's buy lace from a visiting Armenian,
Let's give a beggar a nickel for a bath,
Let's praise Homer to a Homer-sick Athenian,
Let's spread sunbeams all along the path,
Let's go listen to the neighborhood bores,
Let's help mothers through revolving doors,
Let's go to church and fill the plate with money,
Let's tell the minister the sermon was a honey,
Let's teach whales to avoid harpooners,
Let's be kind to congressmen and crooners,
Let's make hunters make friends with moose,
Let's buy songbirds and turn them loose,
And that will teach Nature to tantrum when
My love is speaking to me again.

TWO SONGS FOR A BOSS NAMED
MR. LONGWELL

I

Put it there, Mr. Longwell, put it there!
You're a bear, Mr. Longwell, you're a bear!
It's our verdict
That your service is perfect.
You're a regular American crusader
And you'll lick old H. L. Mencken's Armada.
You know life isn't all a picnic
But it hasn't made you a cynic.
From first to last
As the banner goes past
We'll sing our favorite air.
Our choice always narrows
To the man you can't embarrass,
So put it there, Mr. Longwell, put it there!

II

L for loyalty to his grand old firm,
O for his eyes of blue,
N for his ideals and his spirit of co-operation,
G for his influence on me and you.
W for his ability to collect and co-ordinate facts,
E–L–L for the laborsaving card-index system he put
    through.
Put them all together, they spell LONGWELL,
Which is about what you might expect them to do.

A WARNING TO WIVES

"The outcome of the trial is another warning that if you must kill someone, you should spare the person possessing life insurance. . . . Figures are available to show that convictions are much more common in 'insurance murders' than in other types of homicides." — BOSTON HERALD.

Speak gently to your husband, ma'am,
And encourage all his sneezes;
That nasty cough may carry him off,
If exposed to draughts and breezes.
And suppose the scoundrel lingers on,
And insists on being cured;
Well, it isn't a sin if a girl steps in —
Unless the brute's insured.

Oh, the selfishness of men, welladay, welladay!
Oh the sissies, oh the softies, oh the mice!
Egotistically they strive to keep themselves alive,
And insurance is their scurviest device.
Insurance!
It's insurance
That tries a lady's temper past endurance.
Yet it's safer, on the whole,
To practise self-control
If there's apt to be a question of insurance.

Arsenic soup is a dainty soup,
But not if he's paid his premium.
Or a .32 in a pinch will do,
If you're bored with the epithalemium.

But to make acquittal doubly sure —
No maybes, no perhapses —
You'll do well to wait to expunge your mate
Until his policy lapses.

The hypocrisy of men, welladay, welladay!
Whited sepulchers are much to be preferred.
They claim it's for their wives they evaluate their lives,
But it's fatal if you take them at their word.
Insurance!
Oh, insurance!
What holds potential widows fast in durance?
Not the Adlers and the Freuds,
But the Mutuals and Lloyds,
And the jury's evil mind about insurance.

SONG TO BE SUNG BY THE FATHER OF
INFANT FEMALE CHILDREN

My heart leaps up when I behold
A rainbow in the sky;
Contrariwise, my blood runs cold
When little boys go by.
For little boys as little boys,
No special hate I carry,
But now and then they grow to men,
And when they do, they marry.
No matter how they tarry,
Eventually they marry.
And, swine among the pearls,
They marry little girls.

Oh, somewhere, somewhere, an infant plays,
With parents who feed and clothe him.
Their lips are sticky with pride and praise,
But I have begun to loathe him.
Yes, I loathe with a loathing shameless
This child who to me is nameless.
This bachelor child in his carriage
Gives never a thought to marriage,
But a person can hardly say knife
Before he will hunt him a wife.

I never see an infant (male),
A-sleeping in the sun,
Without I turn a trifle pale

And think Is he the one?
Oh, first he'll want to crop his curls,
And then he'll want a pony,
And then he'll think of pretty girls
And holy matrimony.
He'll put away his pony,
And sigh for matrimony.
A cat without a mouse
Is he without a spouse.

Oh, somewhere he bubbles bubbles of milk,
And quietly sucks his thumbs.
His cheeks are roses painted on silk,
And his teeth are tucked in his gums.
But alas, the teeth will begin to grow,
And the bubbles will cease to bubble;
Given a score of years or so,
The roses will turn to stubble.
He'll sell a bond, or he'll write a book,
And his eyes will get that acquisitive look,
And raging and ravenous for the kill,
He'll boldly ask for the hand of Jill.
This infant whose middle
Is diapered still
Will want to marry
My daughter Jill.

Oh sweet be his slumber and moist his middle!
My dreams, I fear, are infanticiddle.
A fig for embryo Lohengrins!

I'll open all of his safety pins,
I'll pepper his powder, and salt his bottle,
And give him readings from Aristotle.
Sand for his spinach I'll gladly bring,
And Tabasco sauce for his teething ring,
And an elegant, gluttonous alligator
To play with in his perambulator.
Then perhaps he'll struggle through fire and water
To marry somebody else's daughter.

THE PHŒNIX

Deep in the study
Of eugenics
We find that fabled
Fowl, the Phœnix.
The wisest bird
As ever was,
Rejecting other
Mas and Pas,
It lays one egg,
Not ten or twelve,
And when it's hatched,
Out pops itselve.

Waiter, remove yon wistful verse;
It might be better, it might be worse,
But I think that what I am tiredest of
Is poets who write of love.
Love victorious,
Love maltreated,
Love uproarious,
Love defeated,
Love just starting,
Love ethereal,
Love departing,
Love material,
Love eternal,
And, most explicit,
Love infernal
And love illicit.
Love that's slighted
And love Platonic,
Love requited,
Love embryonic,
Love athletic
And love repressed,
Love cosmetic
And love confessed.
I think that what I am tiredest of
Is people who write of love.

I think that what I am tiredest of
Is dramas that drip with love.

Love unspoken,
Love unselfish,
Love just awoken,
Love coy and elfish,
Love tormented,
Love celestial,
Love resented,
Love low and bestial,
Love embarrassed,
Love ambitious,
Love sad and harassed,
Love surreptitious,
Love in Chicago,
Love in China,
In Santiago
And South Carolina,
Love in Manhattan,
Love that rages
In French and Latin
Across the ages.
Waiter, remove yon dripping dramas,
Or bring me a bromide and my old pajamas.

LINES INDITED WITH ALL THE
DEPRAVITY OF POVERTY

One way to be very happy is to be very rich
For then you can buy orchids by the quire and bacon
    by the flitch.
And yet at the same time
People don't mind if you only tip them a dime.
Because it's very funny
But somehow if you're rich enough you can get away
    with spending water like money
While if you're not rich you can spend in one evening
    your salary for the year
And everybody will just stand around and jeer.
If you are rich you don't have to think twice about
    buying a judge or a horse,
Or a lower instead of an upper, or a new suit, or a
    divorce,
And you never have to say When,
And you can sleep every morning until nine or ten,
All of which
Explains why I should like very, very much to be very,
    very rich.

MALICE DOMESTIC

A Mrs. Shepherd of Danbury, Conn.,
She tried to steal our cook,
She may have thought to stay anon.,
But now she's in a book!
Oh — Mrs. — Shepherd,
OH! Mrs. SHEPHERD!
I'll hunt you hither, I'll hunt you yon.
Did you really hope to remain anon.?
Didn't you know the chance you took
Making a pass at a poet's cook?

Oh, Mrs. S. of the Nutmeg State,
No human shame she knew,
Her carnal appetites to sate,
Our home she walked into.
Oh — Mrs. — Shepherd!
OH! Mrs. SHEPHERD!
By hook and by crook and by telephone
You attempted to rape us of our own.
You ruptured the laws of God and man
And made a pass at Matilda Ann.

Then here's a health to Matilda Ann
Whose soups are soundly peppered,
Whose commonest meats are godlike feats,
Who resisted Mrs. Shepherd.
But — Oh — Mrs. — Shepherd!
OH! Mrs. SHEPHERD!

You ruptured the laws of man and God
When in our kitchen you softly trod.
You tiptoed hither, you tiptoed yon,
You fondly hoped to remain anon.,
But householders all, the nation over,
Shall hear the name of the lawless rover
Who by telephone and by hook and crook
Attempted to alienate our cook.
Go back to your home in Danbury, Conn.,
And carry this curse to ponder on:
I hope that your soup is washy-wishy,
Your salad sandy, your butter fishy,
Your oatmeal scorched and your sirloins boiled,
Your soufflé soggy, your sherbet oiled,
Till all your neighbors in Danbury, Conn.,
As they watch the Shepherds grow feeble and wan,
Say: "She should have thought of the chance she took,
Making a pass at a poet's cook."

The bashful Spaniardess apparently finds the amorous
    Spaniard so menacing to her virtue
That she has to employ a duenna so that he shan't
    duennacing to her virtue.

MACHINERY DOESN'T ANSWER, EITHER,
BUT YOU AREN'T MARRIED TO IT

Oh Daddy, look at that man, excuse my pointing, but
    just look at him!

He is in a frenzy or something, as if a red rag or some-
    thing had been shook at him!

His eyes are rolling like a maniac's,

Oh isn't it shocking how insaniacs!

Oh Daddy, he is talking to thin air,

He is having a long conversation with somebody who
    isn't there!

He is talking to himself, he must be under the influence
    of either Luna or Bacchus;

Oh Daddy, Daddy, I think we had better go a long way
    away from him immediately because one in his
    condition might at any moment have an impulse
    to attacchus!

Nay, hush ye, hush ye, do not fret ye, my little white
    manchild,

Who if your parents hadn't been Caucasian would have
    been an ebony or copper or tan child,

Life will teach you many things, chief of which is that
    every man who talks to himself isn't necessarily out
    of his wits;

He may have a wife who knits.

Probably only he and his Maker

Know how many evenings he has spent trying to raise
    a conversation while his beloved created sweaters
    by the acre.

Ah, my inquiring offspring, you must learn that life can
be very bitter,
But never quite so much so as when trying to pry a
word out of a knitter.
Sometimes she knits and sits,
Sometimes she sits and knits,
And you tell her what you have been doing all day and
you ask what she has been doing all day and nothing happens, and you tell her what you would like
to do this evening and ask her what she would
like to do this evening and nothing happens, and
you think you will disintegrate if you don't get
some response, and you speak tenderly of your
courtship and your bridal,
And you might just as well try to get a response out of
an Oriental idol,
And you notice a spasmodic movement of her lips,
And you think she is going to say something but she is
only counting the number of stitches it takes to
surround the hips;
And she furrows her beautiful brow, which is a sign
that something is wrong somewhere and you keep
on talking and disregard the sign,
And she casts a lethal glance, as one who purls before
swine,
And this goes on for weeks
At the end of which she lays her work down and speaks,
And you think now maybe you can have some home
life but she speaks in a tone as far off as Mercury
or Saturn,

And she says thank goodness that is finished, it is a
   sight and she will never be able to wear it, but it
   doesn't matter because she can hardly wait to
   start on an adorable new pattern,
And when this has been going on for a long time, why
   that's the time that strong men break down and go
   around talking to themselves in public, finally,
And it doesn't mean that they are weak mentally or
   spinally,
It doesn't mean, my boy, that they ought to be in an
   asylum like Nijinsky the dancer,
It only means that they got into the habit of talking to
   themselves at home because they themselves were
   the only people they could talk to and get an
   answer.

A CHILD'S GUIDE TO PARENTS

Children, I crave your kind forbearance;
Our topic for today is Parents.

Parents are generally found in couples,
Except when divorce their number quadruples.

Mostly they're married to each other.
The female one is called the mother.

Paternal pride being hard to edit,
The male, or father, claims the credit,

But children, hark! Your mother would rather,
When you arrived, have been your father.

At last on common ground they meet:
Their child is sweetest of the sweet.

But burst not, babe, with boastful glee;
It is themselves they praise, not thee.

The reason Father flatters thee, is —
Thou must be wonderful, aren't thou his?

And Mother admires her offspring double,
Especially after all that trouble.

The wise child handles father and mother
By playing one against the other.

Don't! cries this parent to the tot;
The opposite parent asks, Why not?

Let baby listen, nothing loth,
And work impartially on both.

In clash of wills, do not give in;
Good parents are made by discipline;

Remember the words of the wise old senator:
Spare the tantrum, and spoil the progenitor;

But joy in heaping measure comes
To children whose parents are under their thumbs.

THE TURKEY

There is nothing more perky
Than a masculine turkey.
When he struts he struts
With no ifs or buts.
When his face is apoplectic
His harem grows hectic,
And when he gobbles
Their universe wobbles.

THE SEVEN SPIRITUAL AGES OF
MRS. MARMADUKE MOORE

Mrs. Marmaduke Moore, at the age of ten
(Her name was Jemima Jevons then),
Was the quaintest of little country maids.
Her pigtails slapped on her shoulderblades;
She fed the chickens, and told the truth
And could spit like a boy through a broken tooth.
She could climb a tree to the topmost perch,
And she used to pray in the Methodist church.

At the age of twenty her heart was pure,
And she caught the fancy of Mr. Moore.
He broke his troth (to a girl named Alice),
And carried her off to his city palace,
Where she soon forgot her childhood piety
And joined in the orgies of high society.
Her voice grew English, or, say, Australian,
And she studied to be an Episcopalian.

At thirty our lives are still before us,
But Mr. Moore had a friend in the chorus.
Connubial bliss was overthrown
And Mrs. Moore now slumbered alone.
Hers was a nature that craved affection;
She gave herself up to introspection;
Then, finding theosophy rather dry,
Found peace in the sweet Bahai and Bahai.

Forty! and still an abandoned wife.
She felt old urges stirring to life.
She dipped her locks in a bowl of henna
And booked a passage through to Vienna.
She paid a professor a huge emolument
To demonstrate what his ponderous volume meant.
Returning, she preached to the unemployed
The gospel according to St. Freud.

Fifty! she haunted museums and galleries,
And pleased young men by augmenting their salaries.
Oh, it shouldn't occur, but it does occur,
That poets are made by fools like her.
Her salon was full of frangipani,
Roumanian, Russian and Hindustani,
And she conquered par as well as bogey
By reading a book and going Yogi.

Sixty! and time was on her hands —
Maybe remorse and maybe glands.
She felt a need for a free confession,
To publish each youthful indiscretion,
And before she was gathered to her mothers,
To compare her sinlets with those of others,
Mrs. Moore gave a joyous whoop,
And immersed herself in the Oxford Group.

That is the story of Mrs. Moore,
As far as it goes. But of this I'm sure —
When seventy stares her in the face
She'll have found some other state of grace.

Mohammed may be her Lord and master,
Or Zeus, or Mithros or Zoroaster.
For when a lady is badly sexed
God knows what God is coming next.

Princess Sara Mdvirenikoff
(The former Sally Smith)
She's got her a princeling sure enough,
But nothing to keep him with.
She placed her order in 'twenty-nine,
She bought him at the peak,
And during the recent price decline
The Prince has been — well, bleak.
But the Princess, clinging to love's young dream,
Has been hustling ever since,
And with the aid of a Beauty Cream,
She's thawing out the prince.

How much do you owe
On the old château?
Do you need a bill of divorcement?
Would you like a whirl
With a belted earl? —
Sister, can you spare an endorsement?

Mrs. Ella Louella Pine
Of Cinders Junction, Kan.,
Her matrimonial life is fine
While she supports her man.
Her matrimonial life is gray
When laundry bags are slim,
And during the recent rainy day
Her life was rather grim.

But *Pinkley Pills* have showed her how
To cure that steady ache.
Her picture's in the papers now,
And everything is jake.

Are you on the spot
For lack of a yacht?
Do you need a bill of divorcement?
Would you care to bleach
On a foreign beach?
Sister, can you spare an endorsement?

MONEY IS EVERYTHING

Better a parvenu
Living luxuriously on Park Arvenu
Than a Schuyler or a Van Rensselaer
Living inexpensselaer.

I find it very difficult to enthuse
Over the current news.
The daily paper is so harrowing that it is costly even
  at the modest price of three cents;
It lands on your doorstep with a thud and you can't
  bear to look at it but neither can you forbear, be-
  cause it lies there with all the gruesome fascination
  of something that fell or jumped from the thirtieth
  floor and lit on a picket fence.
And you furtively eye your radio which crouches in the
  corner like a hyena ready to spring,
And you know that what you want is Baby Snooks or
  Dr. I.Q. and you know that what you will get is
  Gabriel Heatter or Raymond Gram Swing.
Wherever you turn, whatever escapist stratagem you
  use,
All you get is news,
And just when you think that at least the outlook is
  so black that it can grow no blacker, it worsens,
And that is why I do not like to get the news, because
  there has never been an era when so many things
  were going so right for so many of the wrong
  persons.

IT ALL DEPENDS ON WHO YOU ARE

I am a kindly man at heart,
Awake to human needs,
A diligent student of the art
Of doing kindly deeds.
I never turn a beggar away
(And don't the beggars know it!)
And every night I quietly pray
To be a better poet.
Yet no reporter grasps his pen
To praise my noble nature,
But prefers perhaps infamouser men
Of famouser nomenclature.

There's Orson Welles,
And Stephen Early,
And the Dardanelles,
And General Hurley,
And Lucille Ball,
And Salvador Dali,
And people who call
Miss Parsons "Lollie,"
And if these or others of the headline ilk
Give an overfed kitten a sip of milk,
The presses whirl
And the newsboys roar,
And the press has recorded one good deed more.

It all depends on who you are;
Yes indeedy, you have said it, it's a fact;

Act kindly; but it's well to be a star,
If expecting any credit for the act.
It is sad,
But true,
That I
And you
Could spend our days in benevolent ways
And a damn would be given by nobody.
Nobody,
No, nobody.
We could guide old ladies across the street,
And stand old ladies to a bite to eat,
And give old ladies a lift to town,
And help old ladies knock the landlord down,
And a damn would be given by nobody.

I am, I've said, a kindly man,
Of less than modest wealth,
And I sometimes tire, as a person can,
Of doing good by stealth.
I frequently go without a meal
That an orphan may have his,
But the lonely inner glow I feel
My only guerdon is.
O, oft I've handed some hag in weeds
My final Camel or Tareyton,
But nobody chronicles the deeds
Of this Forgotten Samaritan.

But there's George Raft,
And Josef Stalin,

And Senator Taft,
And Gracie Allen,
And Mayor Hague,
And Annie Sheridan,
And Vera Vague,
And the Mayor of Meriden,
And if they or others in a similar pickle
Should bestow on the Aga Khan a nickel,
Watch the presses whirl
And the newsboys roar
As the press records one good deed more.

It all depends on who you are;
Yes indeedy, you have said it, it's the truth;
I'd be selfisher and happier by far
Had I learned that simple lesson in my youth.
For it's plain
To see
That you
And me
Could sit up nights over other people's plights,
And a damn would be given by nobody.
Nobody,
No, nobody.
You can rescue old men from the depths of gin
And restore old men to their long-lost kin
You can give old men the coats off your backs
And help old men evade the income tax,
But a damn will be given by nobody
Unless you're somebody.

THE WOMBAT

The wombat lives across the seas,
Among the far Antipodes.
He may exist on nuts and berries,
Or then again, on missionaries;
His distant habitat precludes
Conclusive knowledge of his moods.
But I would not engage the wombat
In any form of mortal combat.

I can't say that I feel particularly one way or the other
    towards bell-boys,

But I do admit that I haven't much use for the it's-just-
    as-well boys,

The cheery souls who drop around after every catas-
    trophe and think they are taking the curse off

By telling you about somebody who is even worse off.

No matter how deep and dark your pit, how dank your
    shroud,

Their heads are heroically unbloody and unbowed.

If you have just lost the one love of your life, there is no
    possible doubt of it,

They tell you there are as good fish in the sea as ever
    came out of it.

If you are fined ten dollars for running past a light when
    you didn't but the cop says you did,

They say Cheer up think of the thousand times you
    ran past them and didn't get caught so you're really
    ten thousand bucks ahead, Hey old kid?

If you lose your job they tell you how lucky you are
    that you've saved up a little wealth

And then when the bank folds with the savings they
    tell you you sure are lucky to still have your health.

Life to them is just one long happy game,

At the conclusion of which the One Great Scorer writes
    not whether you won it or lost it, but how you
    played it, against your name.

Kismet, they say, it's Fate. What is to be, will be. Buck
    up! Take heart!
Kismet indeed! Nobody can make me grateful for Paris
    Green in the soup just by assuring me that it comes
    that way Allah carte.

WINTER COMPLAINT

Now when I have a cold
I am careful with my cold,
I consult my physician
And I do as I am told.
I muffle up my torso
In woolly woolly garb,
And I quaff great flagons
Of sodium bicarb.
I munch on aspirin,
I lunch on water,
And I wouldn't dream of osculating
Anybody's daughter,
And to anybody's son
I wouldn't say howdy,
For I am a sufferer
Magna cum laude.
I don't like germs,
But I'll keep the germs I've got.
Will I take a chance of spreading them?
Definitely not.
I sneeze out the window
And I cough up the flue,
And I live like a hermit
Till the germs get through.
And because I'm considerate,
Because I'm wary,
I am treated by my friends
Like Typhoid Mary.
Now when you have a cold

You are careless with your cold,
You are cocky as a gangster
Who has just been paroled.
You ignore your physician,
You eat steaks and oxtails,
You stuff yourself with starches,
You drink a lot of cockstails,
And you claim that gargling
Is of time a waste,
And you won't take soda
For you don't like the taste,
And you prowl around parties
Full of selfish bliss,
And you greet your hostess
With a genial kiss.
You convert yourself
Into a deadly missile,
You exhale Hello's
Like a steamboat whistle.
You sneeze in the subway
And you cough at dances,
And let everybody else
Take their own good chances.
You're a bronchial boor,
A bacterial blighter;
And you get more invitations
Than a gossip writer.

Yes, your throat is froggy,
And your eyes are swimmy,
And your hand is clammy,

And your nose is brimmy,
But you woo my girls,
And their hearts you jimmy
While I sit here
With the cold you gimmy.

OH TO BE ODD!

Hypochondriacs

Spend the winter at the bottom of Florida and the
summer on top of the Adirondriacs.

You go to Paris and live on champagne wine and cognac
If you're a dipsomognac.

If you're a manic-depressive

You don't go anywhere where you won't be cheered up,
and people say "There, there!" if your bills are ex-
cessive.

But you stick around and work day and night and night
and day with your nose to the sawmill

If you're nawmill.

ADVENTURES OF ISABEL

Isabel met an enormous bear,
Isabel, Isabel, didn't care;
The bear was hungry, the bear was ravenous,
The bear's big mouth was cruel and cavernous.
The bear said, Isabel, glad to meet you,
How do, Isabel, now I'll eat you!
Isabel, Isabel, didn't worry,
Isabel didn't scream or scurry.
She washed her hands and she straightened her hair up,
Then Isabel quietly ate the bear up.

Once in a night as black as pitch
Isabel met a wicked old witch.
The witch's face was cross and wrinkled,
The witch's gums with teeth were sprinkled.
Ho ho, Isabel! the old witch crowed,
I'll turn you into an ugly toad!
Isabel, Isabel, didn't worry,
Isabel didn't scream or scurry,
She showed no rage and she showed no rancor,
But she turned the witch into milk and drank her.

Isabel met a hideous giant,
Isabel continued self-reliant.
The giant was hairy, the giant was horrid,
He had one eye in the middle of his forehead.
Good morning Isabel, the giant said,
I'll grind your bones to make my bread.

Isabel, Isabel, didn't worry,
Isabel didn't scream or scurry.
She nibbled the zwieback that she always fed off,
And when it was gone, she cut the giant's head off.

Isabel met a troublesome doctor,
He punched and he poked till he really shocked her.
The doctor's talk was of coughs and chills
And the doctor's satchel bulged with pills.
The doctor said unto Isabel,
Swallow this, it will make you well.
Isabel, Isabel, didn't worry,
Isabel didn't scream or scurry.
She took those pills from the pill concocter,
And Isabel calmly cured the doctor.

MY DEAR, HOW EVER DID YOU THINK UP
THIS DELICIOUS SALAD?

This is a very sad ballad,
Because it's about the way too many people make a
salad.
Generally they start with bananas,
And they might just as well use Gila monsters or
iguanas.
Pineapples are another popular ingredient,
Although there is one school that holds preserved pears
or peaches more expedient,
And you occasionally meet your fate
In the form of a prune or a date.
Rarely you may chance to discover a soggy piece of
tomato looking very forlorn and Cinderella-ry,
But for the most part you are confronted by apples and
celery,
And it's not a bit of use at this point to turn pale or
break out in a cold perspiration,
Because all this is only the foundation,
Because if you think the foundation sounds unenticing,
Just wait until we get to the dressing, or rather, the
icing.
There are various methods of covering up the body, and
to some, marshmallows are the pall supreme,
And others prefer whipped cream,
And then they deck the grave with ground-up peanuts
and maraschinos
And you get the effect of a funeral like Valentino's,

And about the only thing that in this kind of salad is
    never seen
Is any kind of green,
And oil and vinegar and salt and pepper are at a
    minimum,
But there is a maximum of sugar and syrup and ginger
    and nutmeg and cinnamum,
And my thoughts about this kind of salad are just as
    unutterable
As parsnips are unbutterable,
And indeed I am surprised that the perpetrators haven't
    got around to putting buttered parsnips in these
    salmagundis,
And the salad course nowadays seems to be a month
    of sundaes.

THE SHREW

Strange as it seems, the smallest mammal
Is the shrew, and not the camel.
And that is all I ever knew,
Or wish to know, about the shrew.

WHAT ALMOST EVERY WOMAN KNOWS
SOONER OR LATER

Husbands are things that wives have to get used to put-
     ting up with,
And with whom they breakfast with and sup with.
They interfere with the discipline of nurseries,
And forget anniversaries,
And when they have been particularly remiss
They think they can cure everything with a great big
     kiss.
They are annoying when they stay home
And even more annoying when they roam,
And when you tell them about something they have
     done they just look unbearably patient and smile a
     superior smile,
And think, Oh she'll get over it after a while.
And they always drink cocktails faster than they can
     assimilate them,
And if you look in their direction they act as if they
     were martyrs and you were trying to sacrifice, or
     immolate them.
And when it's a question of walking five miles to play
     golf they are very energetic but if it's doing any-
     thing useful around the house they are very
     lethargic,
And then they tell you that women are unreasonable
     and don't know anything about logic,
And they never want to get up or go to bed at the same
     time as you do,

And when you perform some simple common or garden
rite like putting cold cream on your face or apply-
ing a touch of lipstick they seem to think you are
up to some kind of black magic like a priestess of
Voodoo,

And if you serve meat balls for dinner they look put-
upon and say Can't we ever have a sirloin or a
porterhouse,

So you get them what they want and then when the
bills come in they act as if you were trying to drive
them to the slorterhouse,

And they are brave and calm and cool and collected
about the ailments of the person they have prom-
ised to honor and cherish,

But the minute they get a sniffle or a stomach-ache of
their own, why you'd think they were about to
perish,

And when you are alone with them they ignore all the
minor courtesies and as for airs and graces, they
utterly lack them,

But when there are a lot of people around they hand
you so many chairs and ash trays and sandwiches
and butter you with such bowings and scrapings
that you want to smack them.

Husbands are indeed an irritating form of life,

And yet through some quirk of Providence most of
them are really very deeply ensconced in the affection of their wife.

PRIDE GOETH BEFORE A RAISE
or
AH, THERE, MRS. CADWALLADER–SMITH!

The Cadwallader-Smiths
Are People with Poise;
I consider them one of the minor joys,
Though frequently wishing
That I could share
Their imperturbable savoir-faire.

Madame is a modishly youthful matron,
Artfully dyed and I think enameled;
Monsieur is a generous opera patron,
A Man-about-Town, by trade untrammeled.
Oh the dapper dandies,
The haughty dames,
In the phalanx of hy-
Phenated names!
(Have you ever observed
That the name of Smith
Is the oftenest hy-
Phenated with?)
In the days when they acted namby-pambily
Madame and Monsieur acquired a fambily,
Which accounts for the junior Cadwallader-Smiths,
Those perennial rotogravurian myths,
Maidens who scale the Alps and Rockies,
Debutantes with the world in tow,
Polo players and gentleman jockeys,
And athletes tailored in Savile Row.

Oh glamorous girls and golden boys,
They practically palpitate with poise!
Say me a word. It's a word they've got.
So what?

Well, though hardly copy for a great biographer,
They know how to twinkle for a news photographer.
They don't go to work, but they wallow in shekels,
And they sit on beaches and don't get freckles.
They exchange divorces without bearing malice,
And they all get presented at Buckingham Palace.
They receive reporters with a nonchalant air,
And they're dignified even in the barber chair,
They are dignified even in their testimonials
To beautifying lotions for the crude Colonials.
They take a paper and they read the headlines,
So they've heard of unemployment and they've heard
    of breadlines,
And they philanthropically cure them all
By getting up a costume charity ball.
They own a mansion in the borough of Manhattan
Which they use about as much as Greek and Latin,
And they tipple nectar and they nibble lotus,
And they pay no attention to a jury notus,
And they don't get a summons when they run past
    stop-lights,
So they have the point of view of true cosmopolites.
They could all pay taxes, but they'd rather not.
So what?

Well, they're People with Poise,
The Cadwallader-Smiths,
With the sensitive senses of monoliths,
Which I freely admit
I could use myself,
Had I all I desire of profit and pelf.

When people start saying Hurrah for such and such
     a date you generally find
That they have an ax to grind.
For instance, Mother's Day (formerly May 2nd) comes
     in very handy
For those who support themselves by the sale of flowers
     and candy,
And June 20th, now better known as Father's Day, or,
     in the friendlier ads,
As Dad's,
Is Oh boy what a break
For those who cigars and neckties do make.
And Christmas and Easter and Saint Valentine's Day,
     and, for all I know, the day of Saint Thomas,
Are also given over to commerce
Till indeed it would take a fictional detective
To open a newspaper on any day of the year without
     finding it a Day invented by some live-wire account
     exective.
Well, this scheme may have coerced a lot of people
     who would otherwise have saved their money into
     becoming consumers
But I shall continue to regard it as one of Civilization's
     ugliest tumors,
And I hope that all the advertising agents who had any-
     thing to do with putting it o'er
Get all the diseases and things that they have taken out
     of the bathroom and put into the full pages of
     magazines with a million circulation or more.

THE SQUIRREL

A squirrel to some is a squirrel,
To others, a squirrel's a squirl.
Since freedom of speech is the birthright of each,
I can only this fable unfurl:
A virile young squirrel named Cyril,
In an argument over a girl,
Was lambasted from here to the Tyrol
By a churl of a squirl named Earl.

It is possible that most individual and international social and economic collisions

Result from humanity's being divided into two main
divisions,

Both of which are irreconcilable,

And neither is by the other beguilable;

Their lives are spent in mutual interference,

And yet you cannot tell them apart by their outward
appearance.

Indeed the only way in which to tell one group from
the other you are able

Is to observe them at the table,

Because the only visible way in which one group from
the other varies

Is in its treatment of the cream and sugar on cereal
and berries.

Group A, which we will call the Swozzlers because it
is a very suitable name, I deem,

First applies the sugar and then swozzles it all over the
place pouring on the cream,

And as fast as they put the sugar on they swozzle it
away,

But such thriftlessness means nothing to ruthless ego-
tists like they,

They just continue to scoop and swozzle and swozzle
and scoop,

Until there is nothing left for the Snodgrasses, or second
group.

A Snodgrass is a kind, handsome intelligent person who
    pours the cream on first,
And then deftly sprinkles the sugar over the cereal or
    berries after they have been properly immersed,
Thus assuring himself that the sugar will remain on
    the cereal and berries where it can do some good,
    which is his wish,
Instead of being swozzled away to the bottom of the
    dish.
The facts of the case for the Snodgrasses are so self-
    evident that it is ridiculous to debate them,
But this is unfortunate for the Snodgrasses as it only
    causes the sinister and vengeful Swozzlers all the
    more to hate them.
Swozzlers are irked by the superior Snodgrass intel-
    ligence and nobility
And they lose no opportunity of inflicting on them every
    kind of incivility.
If you read that somebody has been run over by an
    automobile
You may be sure that the victim was a Snodgrass, and
    a Swozzler was at the wheel.
Swozzlers start wars and Snodgrasses get killed in
    them,
Swozzlers sell water-front lots and Snodgrasses get ma-
    laria when they try to build in them.
Swozzlers invent fashionable diets and drive Snod-
    grasses crazy with tables of vitamins and calories,
Swozzlers go to Congress and think up new taxes and
    Snodgrasses pay their salaries,

Swozzlers bring tigers back alive and Snodgrasses get
eaten by anacondas,
Snodgrasses are depositors and Swozzlers are absconders,
Swozzlers hold straight flushes when Snodgrasses hold
four of a kind,
Swozzlers step heavily on the toes of Snodgrasses' shoes
as soon as they are shined.
Whatever achievements Snodgrasses achieve, Swozzlers
always top them;
Snodgrasses say Stop me if you've heard this one, and
Swozzlers stop them.
Swozzlers are teeming with useful tricks of the trade
that are not included in standard university cur-
ricula;
The world in general is their oyster, and Snodgrasses in
particular.
So I hope for your sake, dear reader, that you are a
Swozzler, but I hope for everybody else's sake
that you are not,
And I also wish that everybody else was a nice amiable
Snodgrass too, because then life would be just one
long sweet harmonious mazurka or gavotte.

REFLECTION ON THE FALLIBILITY
OF NEMESIS

He who is ridden by a conscience
Worries about a lot of nonscience;
He without benefit of scruples
His fun and income soon quadruples.

A PARABLE FOR SPORTS WRITERS,
SOCIETY COLUMNISTS, BOND
SALESMEN AND POETS

or

GO GET A REPUTATION

I

Ezra Æsop, at eighty-eight,
He published a volume of verse.
The rhymes were ragged,
The meter wilted,
The prosody prosy,
The stanzas stilted.
But other poets of eighty-eight,
Patriarchal or celibate,
Might — conceivably —
Might — believably —
Might — finally, irretrievably —
Have seized the muse by the horns and tail,
And written a volume worse.
So the red fires burned,
And the banners flew,
And the fat nymphs danced
In the pagan dew,
And the mountains skipped like little lambs,
And editors squandered telegrams,
And over deserts,
And under oceans,
Through Rotary, Red Men, Elks and Yosians,
The word flew East and the word flew West,

Flew with the wings of a durmmer's jest,
That the book of the era, beyond debate,
Was the book by the poet of eighty-eight.
O, Excellent Ezra! the people cried,
He might have doddered,
He might have died,
He might have entered a monastery,
He might have adopted his secretary.
But what did he do?
He studied at home,
Then up and published a slender tome.
So they borrowed early and purchased late
The book by the poet of eighty-eight,
And El Dorado had no bonanzas
Like Ezra Æsop's elderly stanzas.

II

Rosalie Ransome, going on six,
She published a volume, too,
And Heaven pity the heretics
Who neglected to read it through.
For the word was out,
In palace and cot,
Of the teensy, weensy, talented tot,
And gangsters gossiped of Rosalie Ransome,
Who lisped iambics,
And lisped 'em handsome.
The public panted,
The press grew giddy,
At the very thought

Of a lyrical kiddy,
And professors pawned their Shelley and Keats
To purchase Rosalie's youthful feats.

III

A regular poet published a book,
And an excellent book it was,
But nobody gave it a second look,
As nobody often does.
He was going on half-past thirty-five,
So it didn't keep him long alive.

Of a lyrical kiddy,
And professors pawned their Shelley and Keats
To purchase Rosalie's youthful feats.

III

A regular poet published a book,
And an excellent book it was,
But nobody gave it a second look,
As nobody often does.
He was going on half-past thirty-five,
So it didn't keep him long alive.

REFLECTION ON THE FALLIBILITY
OF NEMESIS

He who is ridden by a conscience
Worries about a lot of nonscience;
He without benefit of scruples
His fun and income soon quadruples.

RAVEN, DON'T STAY AWAY FROM MY DOOR
—A CHANT FOR APRIL FIRST

What pleasanter task for All Fools' Day than going
    over all the things you have done before
And don't want to do again never no more, never no
    more, never no more?
Oh softer than the lap of ripples on Innisfree's poetically
    described shore
Is never no more.
Sweeter than the prospect of encountering a dozen
    ladies each as exquisite as Mr. Poe's lost Lenore
Is never no more.
More alluring than an invitation to visit rich and charm-
    ing friends on the Côte d'Or
Is never no more.
Oh let us toy with the comforting but untrue tenet that
    the burnt child dreads the fire that burned him;
Let us each of us dream that the last lesson he had was
    a lesson that really learned him.
I at least refuse to be dissuaded by anyone, even Mrs.
    Luce or Mrs. Post or Dorothy Dix or Petrarch's
    Laura;
On this day of days I shall be a hard-shell, shouting fun-
    damentalist never no maura.
Never no more will I be amiable and humble
And ride in the rumble.
Never no more will I see a lady home downtown when
    I am sleepy and want to go up;

Or drink buttermilk, or sauerkraut juice; or anything at all out of a paper cup;

Or see anybody off on a boat;

Or expect anybody else to like a book or a play on which I happen to particularly dote.

Or underestimate a Slav;

Or say politely No I haven't heard a story, when as a matter of fact I have;

Or let any parent tell me what Sister said to Sonny;

Or play bridge for love, or if it comes to that, for money;

Or get flustered into accepting an invitation I don't want to accept just because I can't think quickly at the telephone;

Or believe that something is better than something else just because it's wrapped in cellophone.

Also, commuting and eating out of doors —

These belong on any list of ideal never no mores.

In conclusion may I say that if this were not a song for the First of April I'd feel very guilty

At daring even to contemplate such a devastatingly delightful impossibilty.

To actually see an actual marine monster
Is one of the things that do before I die I wonster.
Should you ask me if I desire to meet the bashful in-
    habitant of Loch Ness,
I could only say yes.
Often my eye with moisture dims
When I think that it has never been my good fortune
    to gaze on one of Nature's whims.
Far from ever having seen a Gorgon
I haven't even seen the midget that sat in the lap of
    Mr. Morgan.
Indeed it is my further ill fortune or mishap
That far from having seen the midget that sat in it I
    have never even seen Mr. Morgan's lap.
Indeed I never much thought about Mr. Morgan's hav-
    ing a lap because just the way you go into churches
    and notice the stained glass more than the apses
When you think about multi-millionaires you don't
    think about their laps as much as their lapses;
But it seems that they do have laps which is one human
    touch that brings them a little closer to me and you,
And maybe they even go so far as to sometimes have
    hiccups too.
But regular monsters like sea serpents don't have laps
    or hiccups or any other characteristic that is human,
And I would rather see a second-rate monster such as
    a mermaid than a first-rate genius such as John
    Bunyan or Schiaparelli or Schubert or Schumann;

Yes, I would rather see one of the sirens
Than two Lord Byrons,
And if I knew that when I got there I could see Cyclops
    or Scylla and Charybdis or Pegasus
I would willingly walk on my hands from here to Dallas,
    Tegasus,
Because I don't mean to be satirical,
But where there's a monster there's a miracle,
And after a thorough study of current affairs, I have
    concluded with regret
That the world can profitably use all the miracles it
    can get,
And I think life would be a lot less demoralizing,
If instead of sitting around in front of the radio listen-
    ing to torture singers sing torture songs we sat
    around listening to the Lorelei loreleising.

It seems to me that if you must be sociable it is better
to go and see people than to have people come and
see you,

Because then you can leave when you are through.

Yes, the moment you begin to nod

You can look at your watch and exclaim Goodness gracious, it is ten o'clock already, I had no idea it was
so late, how very odd!

And you politely explain that you have to get up early
in the morning to keep an important engagement
with a man from Alaska or Siam,

And you politely thank your host and hostess for the
lovely time and politely say good night and politely
scram,

But when you yourself are the home team and the
gathering is under your own roof,

You haven't got a Manchurian's chance of being aloof.

If you glance at your watch it is grievous breach of
hospitality and a disgrace,

And if you are caught in the midst of a yawn you have
to pretend you were making a face and say Come
on everybody, let's see who can make the funniest
face.

Then as the evening wears on you feel more and more
like an unsuccessful gladiator,

Because all the comfortable places to sit in are being
sat in by guests and you have to repose on the
window sill or the chandelier or the radiator,

And somebody has always brought along a girl who looks like a loaf of raisin bread and doesn't know anybody else in the room,

And you have to go over to the corner where she is moping and try to disperse her gloom,

And finally at last somebody gets up and says they have to get back to the country or back to town again,

And you feebly say Oh it's early, don't go yet, so what do they do but sit down again,

And people that haven't said a word all evening begin to get lively and people that have been lively all evening get their second wind and somebody says Let's all go out in the kitchen and scramble some eggs,

And you have to look at him or her twice before you can convince yourself that anybody who would make a suggestion like that hasn't two heads or three legs,

And by this time the birds are twittering in the trees or looking in the window and saying Boo,

But nobody does anything about it and as far as I know they're all still here, and that's the reason I say that it is better to go and see people than to have people come and see you.

LOOK WHAT YOU DID, CHRISTOPHER!

In fourteen hundred and ninety-two,
Somebody sailed the ocean blue.
Somebody borrowed the fare in Spain
For a business trip on the bounding main,
And to prove to people, by actual test,
You could get to the East by traveling West.
Somebody said, Sail on! Sail on!
And studied China and China's lingo,
And cried from the bow, There's China now!
And promptly bumped into San Domingo.
Somebody murmured, Oh dear, oh dear!
I've discovered the Western Hemisphere.

And that, you may think, my friends, was that.
But it wasn't. Not by a fireman's hat.
Well enough wasn't left alone,
And Columbus was only a cornerstone.
There came the Spaniards,
There came the Greeks,
There came the Pilgrims in leather breeks.
There came the Dutch,
And the Poles and Swedes,
The Persians, too,
And perhaps the Medes,
The Letts, the Lapps and the Lithuanians,
Regal Russians, and ripe Roumanians.
There came the French
And there came the Finns,

And the Japanese
With their formal grins.
The Tartars came,
And the Terrible Turks —
In a word, humanity shot the works.
And the country that should have been Cathay
Decided to be
The U.S.A.

And that, you may think, my friends, was that.
But it wasn't. Not by a fireman's hat.
Christopher C. was the cornerstone,
And well enough wasn't left alone.
For those who followed
When he was through,
They burned to discover something, too.
Somebody, bored with rural scenery,
Went to work and invented machinery,
While a couple of other mental giants
Got together
And thought up Science.
Platinum blondes
(They were once peroxide),
Peruvian bonds
And carbon monoxide,
Tax evaders
And Vitamin A,
Vice crusaders,
And tattletale gray —
These, with many another phobia,

We owe to that famous Twelfth of Octobia.
O misery, misery, mumble and moan!
Someone invented the telephone,
And interrupted a nation's slumbers,
Ringing wrong but similar numbers.
Someone devised the silver screen
And the intimate Hollywood magazine,
And life is a Hades
Of clicking cameras,
And foreign ladies
Behaving amorous.
Gags have erased
Amusing dialog,
As gas replaced
The crackling firelog.
All that glitters is sold as gold,
And our daily diet grows odder and odder,
And breakfast foods are dusty and cold —
It's a wise child
That knows its fodder.
Someone invented the automobile,
And good Americans took the wheel
To view American rivers and rills
And justly famous forests and hills —
But somebody equally enterprising
Had invented billboard advertising.
You linger at home
In dark despair,
And wistfully try the electric air.
You hope against hope for a quizz imperial,

And what do they give you?
A doctor serial.
Oh, Columbus was only a cornerstone,
And well enough wasn't left alone,
For the Inquisition was less tyrannical
Than the iron rules of an age mechanical,
Which, because of an error in '92,
Are clamped like corsets on me and you,
While Children of Nature we'd be today
If San Domingo
Had been Cathay.

And that, you may think, my friends, is that.
But it isn't — not by a fireman's hat.
The American people,
With grins jocose,
Always survive the fatal dose.
And though our systems are slightly wobbly,
We'll fool the doctor this time, probly.

WOODMAN, SPARE NOT THAT
UNDERBRUSH

It may be said of whiskers as it is of microbes that Adam
He had 'em,

So it may well be that microbes and saxophones and
travelogues and such-like are all part of our punish-
ment for original sin,

But of all the punishments surely the most cruel and
unusual is the stuff that constantly percolates
through the masculine chin,

And furthermore it is not only cruel and unusual but
most unfair,

Because women have just as much original sin as men
but their chins don't go around sprouting hair,

Or if they do they are even better off than if they don't
because then they don't have to go out and toil
for their living daily

But just make a lot of money sitting quietly on a platform under the management of Ringling Brothers
and Barnum and Bailey.

Scientists say that whiskers were given to us for protection just like fur for the polar bear and prickles
for the cactus, but that statement won't wash or
cleanse,

Because it seems to me that women's faces need a lot
more protection than men's.

Another unfair thing is that you can and often do get
bald on top,

But your whiskers don't stop.

No, at practically the same moment that you are apply-
ing hair-restorer and massage to your naked apex
with infinite trouble
You have to moil away trying to scrape off a lot of facial
stubble,
And if you finally weary of scraping and say Oh I'll let
it grow instead,
It turns out to be red.
Sometimes after a session with the razor I envy the
luxuriant languorous chins of the ancient Assyrians
and Druids,
But I suppose they had a bad time consuming fluids.
I guess what I would really like would be to lie on a
South Sea island inhaling the aroma of the hibiscus
And never to have any more whiskers.

Let us look into the matter of debt

Which is something that the longer you live, why the
deeper into it you get,

Because in the first place every creditor is their debtor's
keeper,

And won't let you get into debt in the first place unless
you are capable of getting in deeper,

Which is an unfortunate coincidence

Because every debtor who is capable of getting deeper
into debt is attracted only to creditors who will encourage him to get deeper into debt, which is a
most fabulous and unfair You-were-a-creditor-in-
Babylon-and-I-was-a-Christian-debtor Elinor Glyn-
cidence.

Some debtors start out with debts which are little ones,

Such as board and lodging and victual ones;

Other debtors start out by never demanding that their
bills be itemized,

Which means that they are bitten by little creditors upon
the backs of bigger creditors and are so on ad in-
finitumized.

Veteran debtors dabble in stocks,

Or their families get adenoids or appendicitis or pox,

Any of which means that debt is what they get beneather and beneather,

Either to them who told them about the stocks or to
them who administer the chloroform and ether.

Some debts are fun while you are acquiring them,

But none are fun when you set about retiring them,
So you think you will reform, you think instead of sink-
ing into debt you will ascend into credit,
So you live on a budget and save twenty-five per cent of
your salary and cut corners and generally audit and
edit,
And that is the soundest idea yet,
Because pretty soon your credit is so good that you can
charge anything you want and settle down for
eternity into peaceful and utterly irremediable debt.

Some people get savage and bitter when to backbiters
 they refer,
But I just purr.
Yes, some people consider backbiters to be rankest of
 the rank,
But frankly, I prefer them to people who go around
 being frank,
Because usually when you are backbitten behind your
 back you don't know about it and it doesn't leave
 a trace,
But frankness consists of having your back bitten right
 to your face,
And as if that weren't enough to scar you,
Why you are right there in person to scotch the defama-
 tion, and if you don't happen to be able to scotch it,
 why where are you?
Frank people are grim, but genuine backbiters are delightful to have around,
Because they are so anxious that if what they have been
 saying about you has reached your ears you
 shouldn't believe it, that they are the most amiable
 companions to be found;
They will entertain you from sunset to dawn,
And cater encouragingly to all your weaknesses so that
 they can broadcast them later on,
So what if they do gnaw on your spine after enjoying
 your beer and skittles?
I don't blame them the least of jots or tittles,

Because certainly no pastime such diversion lends

As talking friends over analytically with friends,

So what if as they leave your house or you leave theirs
backbiters strip your flesh and your clothes off,

At least it is your back that they bite, and not your nose
off.

I believe in a place for everything and everything in its
place,

And I don't care how unkind the things people say
about me so long as they don't say them to my face.

BIOLOGICAL REFLECTION

A girl whose cheeks are covered with paint
Has an advantage with me over one whose ain't.

I YIELD TO MY LEARNED BROTHER
or
IS THERE A CANDLESTICK MAKER IN THE HOUSE?

The doctor gets you when you're born,
The preacher, when you marry,
And the lawyer lurks with costly clerks
If too much on you carry.
Professional men, they have no cares;
Whatever happens, they get theirs.

You can't say When
To professional men,
For it's always When to they;
They go out and golf
With the big bad wolf
In the most familiar way.
Hard times for them contain no terrors;
Their income springs from human errors.

The butcher you can do without,
Also the jolly baker,
And it's childish sport if you wish to thwart
The plaintive candlestick maker,
For they are not professional men,
And we can spare them now and then.

But the noblest lord is ushered in
By a practising physician,

And the humblest lout is ushered out
By a certified mortician.
And in between, they find their foyers
Alive with summonses from lawyers.

Oh, would my parents long ago
Had memorized this motto!
For then might I, their offspring, buy
A Rolls or an Isotto.
But now I fear I never can,
For I am no professional man.

You can't say When
To professional men,
For it's always When to they;
They were doing fine
In '29,
And they're doing fine today.
One beacon doth their paths illumine,
To wit: To err is always humine.

Consider the man without a watch.

He is like a soda without Scotch.

Of the male character I can quickly give you the gist;

It is the reach for the pocket or the glance at the wrist.

From the moment they are fledglings

Males discipline themselves with timings and schedul-
ings.

Be they lovers, golfers, or railroad engineers,

Time is the essential ingredient in their careers,

And there is nothing more surly

Than a watchless man who doesn't know whether he is
late or early,

And clocks are no good to him because he can't take
them along,

And anyhow a clock is only something that you compare
with your watch and find the clock is several minutes wrong.

If there is one thing that every man thinks how sublime
it is,

It is to know what time it is.

Women don't like watches, they only tolerate them
when they are embedded in brooches or bracelets
or belts,

Or in some way disguised to look like something else.

Yes, it's obvious that women don't like them or need
them,

Because with women's watches you need a microscope
and a map to read them.

Time is something they resent, and they fight it with
    peculiarly feminine resistance;
They refuse to acknowledge its existence.
In this sexual conflict in attitude toward time who am
    I to tip the scales?
I only know that more males wait for females than fe-
    males wait for males.

REFLECTION ON THE PASSAGE OF TIME,
ITS INEVITABILITY AND ITS QUIRKS

*In nineteen hunderd
Jeunes filles wondered.*

Ah woe, woe, woe, man was created to live by the
　　sweat of his brow,

And it doesn't make any difference if your brow was
　　moist yesterday and the day before, you've still got
　　to get it moist again right now,

And you know deep in your heart that you will have
　　to continue keeping it dewy

Right up to the time that somebody at the club says,
　　I suppose we ought to go to what's-his-name's
　　funeral, who won the fifth at Bowie?

That's a nasty outlook to face,

But it's what you get for belonging to the human race.

So far as I know, mankind is the only section of creation

That is doomed to either pers- or ex-piration.

Look at the birds flying around, and listen to them as
　　their voices in song they hoist;

No wonder they sing so much, that haven't got any
　　brows, and if they had they couldn't be bothered
　　keeping them moist.

And bees don't do anything either, bees just have a
　　reputation for industry because they are sharp
　　enough to buzz,

And people hear a bee buzzing and don't realize that
　　buzzing isn't any trouble for a bee so they think
　　it is doing more than it actually does,

So next time you are about to expend some enthusiasm
　　on the bee's wonderful industrial powers,

Just remember that that wonderful bee would die laugh-

ing if you asked it to change places with you and
get its brow moist while you went around spend-
ing the day smelling flowers.
Oh yes, and the flowers, they seem to get along all right
without being overactive,
All they do is sit around looking attractive,
And furthermore, if you can believe all you hear,
They only get up energy enough to do that about once
a year.
Thus we see that if you are botany
Your life is just an everlasting spell of pleasant mo-
notony,
But if you are humanity, it is far from so,
And that is why I exclaim Woe woe woe,
Because I don't see much good in being the highest
form of life
If all you get out of it is a brow moist from perpetual
struggle and strife.
Indeed sometimes when my brow is particularly moist
I think I would rather be a humble amœba
Than Solomon in all his glory entertaining the Queen
of Sheba.

HEARTS OF GOLD

or

A GOOD EXCUSE IS WORSE THAN NONE

There are some people who are very resourceful
At being remorseful,
And who apparently feel that the best way to make
    friends
Is to do something terrible and then make amends.
They come to your party and make a great hit with
    your Victorian aunt and with her freely mingle,
And suddenly after another drink they start a lot of
    double entendre the entendre of which is unfortu-
    nately not double but single,
And if you say anything to them they take umbrage,
And later when you are emptying the ash trays before
    going to bed you find them under the sofa where
    they have crept for a good night's slumbrage.
Then next day they are around intoning apologies
With all the grace and conviction of a high-paid choir
    intoning doxologies.
There are people in every group
Who will jog your elbow at table just when you are
    lifting a spoonful of very hot soup,
Or at a musicale or something while you're listening
    to a ravishing obbligato
Will forget their cigarettes and burn a hole in your
    clothes the size of a medium-sized tomato.
And then you are presented with a lot of form-fitting
    apologies

Quite good enough, I am sure, for inclusion in one of the higher-class anthologies.

Everybody says these people have hearts of gold,

But nevertheless they're always talking when you're putting, or splashing mud on you from their car, or giving you a cold,

And they are always sure that today you don't mind their inflicting on you any sorrow,

Because they'll give you so much pleasure when they smilingly apologize tomorrow,

But I myself would rather have a rude word from someone who has done me no harm

Than a graceful letter from the King of England saying he's sorry he broke my arm.

INTROSPECTIVE REFLECTION

*I would live all my life in nonchalance and insouciance
Were it not for making a living, which is rather a
nouciance.*